WHY . . . do some experts now rate Steve Carlton as the equal of any all-time left-hander?

WHAT . . is the prime reason that Hank Aaron usually hits his home runs off baseball's best pitchers?

HOW . . . does Boston's Carlton Fisk compare with Cincinnati's Johnny Bench as a hitter and receiver?

WHO . . . is baseball's brightest new star?

WHEN . . did Dick Allen realize that he had found his happy home in Chicago?

The answers to these and hundreds of other up-to-the-second diamond puzzlers are all featured in this exciting edition of BASEBALL STARS OF 1973. In these intimate, revealing and dramatic stories of baseball's top performers, written by America's best sportswriters, you can relive the unforgettable moments of the thrill-packed 1972 season, and tune in to a new, spectacular 1973 campaign.

BASEBALL
STARS of 1973

edited by RAY ROBINSON

PYRAMID BOOKS NEW YORK

BASEBALL STARS OF 1973

A PYRAMID BOOK

First printing, March 1973

Copyright © 1973 by Ray Robinson

All Rights Reserved

ISBN 0-515-02972-6

Printed in the United States of America

Pyramid Books are published by Pyramid Communications, Inc.
Its trademarks, consisting of the word "Pyramid" and the portrayal
of a pyramid, are registered in the United States Patent Office.

Pyramid Communications, Inc., 919 Third Avenue, New York, N.Y. 10022

CONTENTS

APPENDICES

PREFACE

About half-way through the last World Series I suddenly found myself rooting for the Oakland Athletics. I am not quite sure why this happened and have been trying, ever since, to deduce the reason for this quirk of behavior.

As a lifetime National League fan, and as someone who has, at one time or another, been emotionally attached to the fortunes of the Brooklyn Dodgers, the New York and then the San Francisco Giants—and as a New Yorker who experienced a youthful flirtation with the Cincinnati Reds, vintage 1939 and 1940, when Bucky Walters, Paul Derringer, Billy Werber and Ernie Lombardi were Galahads of my imagination, here I was applauding shamelessly for Mr. Finley's tomentose menagerie.

Such a temporary aberration, I assured myself, had absolutely nothing to do with any latent admiration for the dubious paternalism of Mr. Finley or for his scatter-shot philosophy, although I had to admit that I did feel partial to his proposal to introduce orange colored baseballs into the game. (I have always been able to hit a yellow tennis ball better than the traditional white one; thus, I figured that the orange ball would do wonders in immediately raising the batting averages of all of my favorite players. Could it, for instance, keep Willie Mays around for another year or two? Would yellow baseballs help Hank Aaron break Babe Ruth's home run record?)

Did this transient shift of my loyalties to the Athletics reflect a resentment of the fact that, having heard that Pete Rose of the Reds wears a Spiro Agnew T-shirt under his baseball blouse, I was now totally unprepared to root for his Cincinnati team? After all, since Rose is such a dedicated fury of a player, could I really put him down for his politics? And, certainly, wouldn't it be unfair for me to penalize his teammates for Rose's occasional lapses of thoughtfulness?

So why, then, as a chronic National League fan, was I sitting in front of my television set cheering ardently for Oakland's one-run victories, its anonymous pinch-hitters and for a cast of characters that appeared to have been assembled by producer Joe Papp for his summer plays in New York's Central Park?

Well, I kept telling myself, the times, indeed, have changed. Attitudes have changed. Old loyalties have been shaken, uprooted and forgotten. Even baseball announcers have changed. For example, Ralph Kiner, the former home run slugger who does a rather respectable job of broadcasting the New York Mets games, violated the bounds of propriety one day last year, when he ruthlessly commented on an umpire's strike call, while San Francisco's Juan Marichal was pitching.

"With calls like that," said Ralph, "a pitcher could last a lifetime!" Howard Cosell makes a living saying things like that. But Ralph Kiner?

So, I imagine, if people like Ralph Kiner can alter their stereotypes, so can I. If I was once a chauvinistic, chronic, utterly maniacal National League supporter, I confess I am no longer. Secretly now, I find myself hoping that the once-hated New York Yankees return to their winning glories of yesteryear. Previously bored, enraged and disgusted with Yankee omnipotence, I pine for them to win ball games with puny bunts, relief pitching and defense.

Yes, I suppose the reason for my shift in allegiance is that many of the old loyalties have been loosened—whether they be to baseball clubs, political parties, geographical regions, colleges, restaurants, television networks, movie stars or even—and this is the saddest note of all—to old friends, who have moved away or have disappeared from the orbit of one's daily existence.

In time, perhaps, does this mean that the old devotion to baseball, which seems to be struggling for survival in the affections of many of us, will diminish, too?

I wonder about this, as the new season of 1973 dawns—and as old stars fade away and home town ties give way to the often predatory commercial instincts of management.

I choose to believe baseball will manage to prevail, despite TV saturation (which is also beginning to afflict professional football) and the destruction of the illusion that owners always think first of their fans and players and that players always think first of their fans.

Of one thing I am reasonably certain, however. My dalliance with Oakland's green-and-gold legions was as ephemeral as the five-cent cup of coffee or the nickel cigar. As this summer wears on—and as the pennant races warm up, I will, I'm certain, be rooting for the Giants or the Mets to win a few or for Willie Mays to hit at least one more homer.

But in the 1973 World Series? Who knows? I may find myself again urging the American League team on to victory—for any number of eccentric, private reasons.

Old loyalties? I still have them—but.

RAY ROBINSON
New York City

HANK AARON

41 To Go

by DAN SCHLOSSBERG

In 1973, for the first time, Babe Ruth's all-time home run total of 714, the most revered record in all of sport, is in serious danger.

Ruth's challenger is a most unlikely slugger, a trim 180-pound six-footer, who, until recently, was better known for his batting average than his home run total.

Henry Louis Aaron for many years held the highest average among active players. But it wasn't until he hit 47 home runs at age 37 in 1971 that anyone thought he could catch Babe Ruth.

After the incredible 1971 season pushed his total to 639, Hank Aaron, an unheralded superstar for years, suddenly became a super-celebrity.

The Braves signed him to a three-year contract calling for $200,000 per season, the most ever awarded a baseball player. Atlanta front-office executive Paul Richards flatly stated that Aaron would hit No. 715 on Aug. 31, 1973.

And everyone from Willie Mays—passed in lifetime homers by Aaron in 1972—to Aaron's doctor predicted that someday soon Aaron would break the record, though probably not as soon as Richards had suggested.

Aaron himself reacted to the sudden spotlight by admitting he had his sights set on Ruth. He was, he said, swinging for the fences.

The two-week strike at the start of the 1972 season, however, set back most of the hitters, especially the veterans. Aaron endured an early 5-for-50 slump, the worst of his career, and never really recovered. His final average, .266, was 13 points lower than he had ever batted before.

"I thought at one point that I was about to start hitting," he said, "but I wasn't consistent and I am definitely disappointed in my final average.

"But I figure my main jobs have always been knocking in and scoring runs, not hitting for average. I don't think there's anything wrong with my reflexes, but I have had a tendency to get tired. I've been over-tired a couple of times and it took awhile to bounce back. I hope to rest more in 1973."

He still swatted 34 homers—fourth in the league—and knocked in 77 runs for the Braves, while batting just 448 times. He never lost the respect of such rivals as Cincinnati Reds manager Sparky Anderson.

In the eighth inning of a tie game with two outs and a man at third for the Braves, Anderson ordered Aaron walked intentionally.

"I'm not going to let Hank Aaron beat me in that situation," Anderson said later. "I wouldn't care if he had retired and came down out of the stands to hit, I would have walked him. He lives for those kind of situations."

Another rival pilot, Montreal's Gene Mauch, says, "I'll tell you this about him: we still feel the same way about him as we did 15 years ago. Any pitch above the belt is next door to disaster."

Claude Osteen, who won 20 for Los Angeles in 1972, has a good reason to be wary of Aaron; he's the only active pitcher to have yielded more than a dozen Aaron home run balls.

"If I can win and give up a home run to Aaron, I really don't care," Osteen admitted. "But I would be very nervous if I were facing Aaron when he was going for his record home run. I'd pitch in my normal manner, though. If you're too careful, you often end up throwing the ball right down the middle."

Like Aaron, Babe Ruth slammed 34 homers at age 38, but fell to 22 at age 39 in 1934. Aaron celebrated his 39th birthday last Feb. 5. Unlike Ruth, the gargantuan Yankee, Aaron has the ideal physical build to continue his hot pursuit of the sacrosanct record this season.

In National League history, only Aaron has topped the 40-homer mark seven times. If Bad Henry—N.L. pitchers call him that—can extend that record to eight in 1973, and add one more homer, he and Ruth will be in a flat-footed tie for the all-time home run crown. Aaron, with 673, is 41 away.

Physically, Aaron seems primed for the 1973 season. He's remained remarkably free of injuries since suffering a broken ankle in September of 1954, his rookie season. More recently, he's been bothered by a knee injury suffered in a 1970 home-plate collision and a nagging neck pain discovered in 1971. Rest and heat treatments have relieved both ailments, however.

"I won't punish myself just to go after Ruth's record," says Aaron. "I mean not only physically punish but also mentally. For instance, I would never let my personal ambition to go after another man's record cause me to lose the respect of the fans and press. I couldn't stand to hear them say that I was hurting the team by hanging around just going after that record."

The Braves' medical consultant, Dr. Robert Wells, is confident Aaron can eclipse Ruth's record in the near future.

"He looks at least six or seven years younger than he is," says Dr. Wells of Aaron. "He is a strong, vigorous man. From a medical standpoint, he's one of the lesser problems on the Braves. I expect he will have recurrent minor medical problems, but I don't foresee any major medical problems that would keep him from breaking Babe Ruth's record. Also, let me point out that he's extremely stable emotionally—despite all the pressure he's under."

Aaron used to be one of the most congenial interviews in the game, and still is strictly a gentleman in dealing with the press. At times, though, the strain of answering the same question a dozen times a day shows through his attitude.

"Oh, the newsmen," he insists. "they don't bother me."

In addition to the extra writers who'll be following his exploits this season, NBC will put the television spotlight on Aaron when he nears the record—even if it means cutting into its prime-time schedule of new shows in fall, 1973.

"Sure I think about the record," says Aaron, who hears of nothing else from his interviewers. "I think I can make it if I stay healthy and if I have a strong man batting behind me so they won't pitch around me."

Since the Braves are loaded with hitters, Aaron should have no problem getting plenty of good pitches to hit. There's bound to be a slugger following him in the lineup.

There's a third factor involved in Aaron's race with The Babe; he wants his homers to count for something.

A good pennant race in 1973 would give Aaron that extra incentive.

"I have to be motivated by something other than the record," the veteran slugger suggests. "That just isn't enough. Fifteen years ago, I didn't need it. Now I do. I need to have an overwhelming responsibility that will keep me in the lineup as often as possible. Lots of things motivate a player. But nothing does it like the chance for a championship."

Aaron, a standout in the 1957 Braves' World Championship, has played on generally good Braves teams, and was disappointed when the 1972 club finished fourth in the six-team Western Division. In addition to 1957, Aaron played with a league champion in 1958, and was a key cog on the 1959 and 1969 clubs which lost playoffs which would have led to the World Series.

Henry Aaron became a Brave in 1952 when scout Dewey Griggs bought his contract for $10,000 from the old Indianapolis Clowns. Even then, he was an outstanding prospect, though his cross-handed batting style defied all the rules of hitting. In those days, Aaron was an infielder, playing second and short, though he adapted well to the outfield and later earned Gold Glove awards for his defensive play in right field.

When Griggs signed him, no one dared think of the skinny kid from Mobile, Ala. as a home run threat.

"When I broke in, I wasn't even a power hitter," Aaron remembers. "I weighed 160 and hit a total of nine home runs at Eau Claire (Wis.). It wasn't much to get excited over."

When he followed that 1952 season with a .362 average, 22 homers, and 125 RBI at Jacksonville (Sally), he won a trip to Milwaukee and got a chance as a regular when Bobby Thomson broke his leg in spring training. Aaron hasn't been out of the lineup since.

He's led the National League in every major batting category—hitting, homers, and runs batted in—at least twice. Four times, he's matched his uniform—No. 44—in home runs. Taking the best output in each area, Aaron can show a .355 average (1959), 47 homers (1971), and 132 RBI (1957). He was voted the N.L.'s Most Valuable Player in 1957 and *The Sporting News*' Player of the Year in 1963.

That's quite a track record for a "wrist hitter" who does things so well and so naturally that at one time he was accused of "falling asleep" at the plate.

Aaron holds such a laundry list of National and major league batting records that they are too numerous to mention. Among other things, he's the all-time champ in total bases, one of two players with 3,000 hits and 500 homers (Willie Mays is the other), and one of five men ever to hit more than 30 homers and steal more than 30 bases in the same season (1963).

The record which explains Aaron's secret to success is most years with 30 or more homers—14. Even the great Babe Ruth did not have 14 seasons over the 30 mark. The American League slugging king accomplished the feat 13 times, one less than Aaron.

Thus Aaron's secret is consistency. Only in 1972, when he batted 448 times, and in his injury-shortened rookie year of 1954, did he have less than 495 at-bats in a season.

And not only does he play often, but he plays well—at several positions. He often filled in as an infielder after coming up to Milwaukee in 1954, then converted to first base from the outfield on a full-time basis in mid-1971.

It appears, however, that Aaron's outfielding days are at an end, although the fans keep voting him onto the N.L. All-Star team at that position. He's been a leading vote-getter in the three seasons since the vote has been restored to the fans, starting in 1970.

Aaron has been an All-Star every year he's been in the majors with the single exception of his rookie season. Oddly, he'd never hit an All-Star homer before 1971, when he connected against fireballer Vida Blue at Detroit.

But Hank's most dramatic All-Star contribution came last year, on his home turf. At Atlanta Stadium July 25, the Nationals trailed 1-0 in the sixth, when Aaron came to bat with a man on base. Tough Gaylord Perry, former National League Cy Young Award winner with a good career record against Aaron, was trying to protect the A.L.'s slim lead. Both men remembered that Perry had yielded Aaron's 600th homer on April 27, 1971.

This time, Perry and Aaron, two righthanded veterans at the peak of their professions, faced each other in the humid Georgia night. Perry threw, and Aaron lofted a line drive over the left-center field fence, putting the N.L. ahead, 2-1.

The fans went wild and even the mild-mannered Aaron admitted later, "I was flying. If I was to have a good All-Star game, I'm glad it came here in Atlanta for the fans. The people in Atlanta have been great to me. They came to see me hit one, and I was pleased to come through."

Light-hitting Cookie Rojas ruined Aaron's party by putting the A.L. ahead again, 3-2, with a two-run shot, but the Nationals tied it in the ninth and won it in the tenth. Joe Morgan, whose single knocked in the winning run, got the game's MVP trophy.

"When Aaron hit the homer, it was like watching a Hollywood movie," said Morgan in the winners' clubhouse. "I thought *he* should be the hero."

The Braves' slugger accepted the kind words as he always does—with modesty. He is as soft-spoken today, at the height of his success, as he was when he broke in nearly two decades ago. He is the quiet leader of a ballclub that is rebuilding with youth, hoping to regain the glory of the late '50s.

Since he is 39, Aaron today requires more rest than he used to, but he still enjoys the game.

"When I came into baseball," he says, "I had a taste for it in my mouth and that has never changed. I still love to play, though it gets harder with the length of the schedule, the traveling, and the night games.

"My main thought at this time is to keep my health and be able to play. In my mind, a hitter is always able to hit, but first he must be fit and able to get on the field to play. Thankfully, I am in good health and my knee is fine. More than thinking about breaking records, I am thinking about playing baseball. That is primary in my mind.

"First you play baseball, then you play to win, and then you try for home runs. The understanding of the fans is important. The pressure comes from the stands."

Atlanta Manager Eddie Mathews, who combined with Aaron to hit a record 863 homers as teammates, understands the pressure. Mathews, like Aaron, was once the game's premier power hitter.

"He takes everything in stride," the ex-third baseman says of Aaron. "He's consistent as far as right or lefthanded pitching goes. A pitcher who throws off-speed pitches—slow curves or change-ups—will probably give him a little more trouble than the guy who brings it real good."

Aaron's leading victims include some outstanding hurlers. Tops on the list is Don Drysdale, former star righthander of the Los Angeles Dodgers. Big D yielded 17 of Aaron's 673 homers. Among active pitchers, Claude Osteen, Bob Gibson, Larry Dierker, Steve Carlton, Steve Blass, and Juan Marichal all have given up at least five Aaron homers.

"The reason I hit most of my home runs off these guys," Aaron explained, "is we see them every series we play against their clubs. They pitch to me like they'd pitch to anyone else. They go with their best stuff and hope they can get me out. The good pitchers are certainly going to have their days against you, but if you're a good hitter, you'll have your days against them."

Aaron has made it clear he wants a front-office job when his playing career is over, and many baseball people think he might make a good general manager.

"Hank would be good at whatever he decides to do," says Earl Williams, Atlanta's former slugging catcher, summing up the general feeling about Aaron's capabilities. "If he wants to manage or be a general manager, he'd be good at it."

For now, though, he's very much a ballplayer—one of the best.

"His swing is just as smooth and effective as it ever was," says Mathews. "He never seems to slow down. Hank does the job today exactly as he has since coming to the Braves."

Fergie Jenkins, who's won 20 for the Cubs in each of the last six seasons, maintains due respect for Aaron's bat.

"Just when you've thrown the ball by him," Jenkins reports, "he's got that bat around so fast he almost takes the ball out of the catcher's glove. I won't throw him too many fastballs, no siree."

There is some controversy about the Aaron-Ruth race and the climb to 714 homers. Old-timers say Ruth was really better because he hit his 714 in 8,399 times at bat, while Aaron has already been up more than 11,000 times for his 673 homers to date.

But the pro-Aaron crowd says Ruth did not have to cope with night ball, exhausting coast-to-coast travel, the emergence of many relief specialists, 11 opposition teams instead of seven, plus constant exposure in the mass media.

Also, Ruth had the good fortune to spend most of his career in Yankee Stadium, where his lefthanded swing and the 296-foot right-field line were meant for each other and nicknamed "the House that Ruth Built." While Aaron has played in good hitters' parks in both Milwaukee and Atlanta, neither has the short dimensions Ruth enjoyed.

To Aaron, Ruth will always be the home run king. "He'll still be the best, even if I pass him," the Braves' star emphasized. "Even if I am lucky enough to hit 715 home runs, Babe Ruth will still be regarded as the greatest home run hitter who ever lived."

But to Braves' fans, all they know is 673 down, 41 to go.

DAN SCHLOSSBERG, self-styled "baseball fanatic," is the author of an upcoming book, "Let's Talk About Baseball." He is also a newspaper writer and editor based in New Jersey.

HANK AARON

Year	Club	Lea	Pos	AB	R	H	HR	RBI	Avg.
1952	Eau Claire	Northern	SS	345	79	116	9	61	.336
1953	Jacksonville	So. Atl.	2B	574	115	208	22	125	.362
1954	Milwaukee	N. L.	OF	468	58	131	13	69	.280
1955	Milwaukee	N. L.	OF-2B	602	105	189	27	106	.314
1956	Milwaukee	N. L.	OF	609	106	200	26	92	.328
1957	Milwaukee	N. L.	OF	615	118	198	44	132	.322
1958	Milwaukee	N. L.	OF	601	109	196	30	95	.326
1959	Milwaukee	N. L.	OF-3B	629	116	223	39	123	.355
1960	Milwaukee	N. L.	OF-2B	590	102	172	40	126	.292
1961	Milwaukee	N. L.	OF-3B	603	115	197	34	120	.327
1962	Milwaukee	N. L.	OF-1B	592	127	191	45	128	.323
1963	Milwaukee	N. L.	OF	631	121	201	44	130	.319
1964	Milwaukee	N. L.	OF-2B	570	103	187	24	95	.328
1965	Milwaukee	N. L.	OF	570	109	181	32	89	.318
1966	Atlanta	N. L.	OF-2B	603	117	168	44	127	.279
1967	Atlanta	N. L.	OF-2B	600	113	184	39	109	.307
1968	Atlanta	N. L.	OF-1B	606	84	174	29	86	.287
1969	Atlanta	N. L.	OF-1B	547	100	164	44	97	.300
1970	Atlanta	N. L.	OF-1B	516	103	154	38	118	.298
1971	Atlanta	N. L.	1B-OF	495	95	162	47	118	.327
1972	Atlanta	N. L.	1B-OF	448	75	119	34	77	.266
	World Series								
1957	Milwaukee	N. L.	OF	28	5	11	3	7	.393
1958	Milwaukee	N. L.	OF	27	3	9	0	2	.333

DICK ALLEN

Chisox Colossus

by WILLIAM BARRY FURLONG

It was September and the late Summer shadows in Yankee Stadium had retreated before the oncoming night. He had never been with a pennant-winner and as Dick Allen of the Chicago White Sox stepped into the batter's box against the New York Yankees the frail ghosts of victory still flitted about the edges of the Grail called hope. At that point, the White Sox—for so long an abused and futile team—still had a hope of winning the title in the Western Division in the American League. The knowledge sustained Dick Allen—and frightened the Yankee fans. In the bleachers, as he came to bat, some of them unfurled a banner that captured their feelings:

"SAVE OUR MONUMENTS! WALK ALLEN!"

The realism was in what Allen had done to Yankee pitching in 1972. He smashed the best Yankee pitcher, reliever Sparky Lyle, for a ninth-inning three run homer that won one game. Just a week earlier he'd won another game with a monumental 470-foot drive into the distant center-field bleachers in White Sox park, where only three men had hit a baseball in the previous 60 years.

The symbolism was in what Dick Allen had suddenly come to mean in 1972. No longer was he the "bad boy" of ruined potential. Instead he was an electrifying colossus who had come to dominate the American league—for this one season—as had no man since The Babe.

The awards began pouring in—the all-star team, the Most Valuable Player award—and so did the hyperbole: no man could hit so hard so often (he led the league in homers and runs batted in) and carry an entire ball-

19

club—virtually alone, on his own shoulders—to a contending position in the pennant race. It was all the more intense because of the "trouble" he'd seen in previous years: now he seemed like a swashbuckling throwback to those distant days when the Babe Ruths, the Grover Cleveland Alexanders and the Ty Cobbs dominated the game. He was still setting his own precedents—he didn't go to Spring training in 1972 and he only occasionally bothered with batting practice once the season was well under way. To some there was danger in all this—a looseness and lack of discipline that presaged danger. To others, there was hope—Dick Allen looked like nothing so much as a proud, free spirit, a remnant of independence in a game gone uptight.

Indeed, there are many in baseball who do not want to see the game dominated or infiltrated by a free spirit such as Allen. For the fear is that he's so good that he'll become—as The Babe did—bigger than the game itself. He has skills for it: power, consistency, clutch hitting. He also has the personality for it: independence, an unfettered gift—perhaps even a genius—for crushing egos and establishing the indisputable supremacy of his own being.

Last year the fans swarmed to see him swing. The White Sox drew 1,186,018 to Comiskey park, which is almost triple what they drew to the same ballpark—sans Allen—only two years earlier. Bill Veeck, the one-time genius of front-office action—lamentably retired for these past ten years—estimated that the "crowd-pleasing, crowd-drawing" Dick Allen was worth $750,000 in extra income to the White Sox last year: extra season tickets sold, extra income from concessions all balanced against the extra cost of Allen's salary ($135,000 a year). And this speaks nothing of what Allen—by his own bravura and the way he inspired the White Sox into a critical role in the flag race—did in attracting fans and dollars, into enemy ballparks: The White Sox drew 936,579 on the road. When it's all added up: Dick Allen meant $1-to-$1½ million in income to American League owners that they didn't have just one year earlier.

To the White Sox, he meant more than dollars. He meant survival—and hope. Here was a team that lost 106 games—50 losses more than it won—in 1970. In 1972, with Dick Allen, here was a team that won—in a strike-shortened season—20 more games than it lost.

That's a turnaround of 70 games in the won-lost column—and it was all accomplished within two seasons. That fact alone was important to baseball: in a time when pro football had captured the public imagination—with its dramatic rise of contenders from hitherto last place teams—the "national game" had to establish that it also could make a contender out of a chronic loser. And what it took was Allen who drove in the winning run in 19 games.

To be sure, it was not Allen alone. There was a knuckleball pitcher named Wilbur Wood. And there was a manager named Chuck Tanner, the American League Manager of the Year.

Tanner had his own genius. He took over a demoralized, defeated ball club at the end of the 1970 season and he turned it completely around. His genius was limned and reflected in Allen's genius but it is difficult to say which man's was the greater.

For Tanner discovered one of the elusive secrets of baseball in his handling of Dick Allen: he discovered how to get the most from a ballplayer who had the most to offer. It was a rare and laudable skill, for Dick Allen had trouble as well as triumph to offer.

The trouble was what made him famous. He'd come up to the Philadelphia Phillies in the early 1960's touted as the best-endowed baseball player in the history of western civilization. He'd tried to win the pennant in Philadelphia almost single-handedly: he'd hit a fantastic homer in a key game in 1964, hit others all through the stretch—and still the Phils lost ten in a row at season's end, blew a six-game lead and finished a game out of first place. Thereafter, it seemed that it was not the Phils who were at fault; it was Dick Allen. Philadelphia is a city that was against the Declaration of Independence—indeed, it still may be—and that welcomed the British who drove out the independent thinkers. That is the way they looked at Dick Allen: he was accused of everything except breathing regularly—of drinking, of ignoring batting practice, of paying more attention to his horses than to the horsehides. He met natural disasters (he hit under .300 half the time) and unnatural ones: he cut his hand seriously when he stuck it through an auto headlight while trying to push his car. The result: his throwing hand was so seriously injured that he no longer could play third base and had to be shifted over to first base. But nothing helped him in Philadelphia: it was the kind of a place where he learned to wear his batting helmet all the time for fear of getting brained by a brickbat. Or a brick.

Six years passed—six years of increasing desperation—and the Phils traded him to St. Louis. One year and St. Louis traded him to Los Angeles. One year and Los Angeles traded him to the White Sox. Four teams in four years—and always the aura of trouble that followed him.

Until he got to the White Sox.

Then it was triumph all the way.

The triumph was apparent in the headlines: SOX WIN, ALLEN SLUGS PAIR ... ALLEN BLAST FULFILLS PROPHECY ... SUPERMAN ALLEN HERO AGAIN ... ALLEN, WOOD, LEAD SOX INTO FIRST PLACE ... SOX ROMP, ALLEN HITS 37TH.

The triumph was apparent in the comments of his colleagues:

—Said Blue Moon Odom of the Oakland Athletics: "The main thing with the White Sox is Allen. If you can get him out, you can control the game."

—Said Kansas City pitcher Al Fitzmorris (when told that Allen hit only two homers after 9 p.m. all year): "I don't care what time it is when he comes to bat. I wouldn't give him a pitch to hit if he was batting under a street light."

—Said White Sox manager Tanner: "Dick Allen is doing more for the White Sox this year than any player I have ever seen do for another team. He's doing it all—at bat, in the field, and on the bases."

The triumph was apparent also in the statistics. Allen led the American League in home runs (37) and runs batted in (113), he was third in batting-average—behind Rod Carew of Minnesota (.316)—with a .308 mark.

"I've hit .300 four different times (Ed. note: now five times) but any average I got didn't mean anything if we didn't win," he said last summer. "I know I could push my average way up if I wanted to play for the average instead of the wins."

How?

By protecting himself in the run-potential situations. Not to go for the meaningless single—that builds the average—instead of persisting for the big blow that will mean a victory for the team. "For instance, when we're on the road and it's late in the game and we're tied or one-run down I'm not going to waste my time trying to bleed my way onto first base," he says. "I'm going to try to get that run in that we need." That means he'll be swinging hard at pitches outside the strike zone, instead of waiting-out the pitcher for a walk or a good pitch that he can nick and still get a single on. That's the only way he knows how to go: he's got to be swinging, not walking, in order to perform his particular role for the White Sox.

What are the statistics that reflect how well the slugger does his job?

Here is the mix with which to work: Allen's batting average of .308, his 37 home runs, his 113 runs batted in, his 90 runs scored, even his 19 stolen bases (in 14 tries)—there aren't many sluggers who steal so often to get into scoring position.

From all this, it can be determined that:

—Allen produced 166 runs for the White Sox, more than any other batter produced for any other team in the league.

—His run-production amounted to 29.3 percent of all the runs scored by the White Sox.

—Allen got almost one home run in every four times he got a hit—23.7 percent of the hits were homers. No other regular in the league came close.

—Every time he got a hit, Allen did more than produce a run—which is a signal of exceptional clutch hitting. His final average was 1.064 runs for every hit. Nobody else in the American League even came close to producing a run-per-hit—which is the ultimate measure of how well Allen does his job.

Allen grew up in Wampum, Pa., as one of nine children of Mrs. Era Allen, who gave them all the values—even if she didn't have much money—that are enduring. Dick has always had a powerful sense of family: when he was signed to a bonus of a reported $50,000 back in 1959, he used half of it to buy a new home for his mother. He also sought—and got—a chance in Organized Baseball for one of his brothers and made it a condition of his contract that yet another brother be given a chance as a scout in the Phillies' farm system. That attitude endures today: to sign him last season, the White Sox agreed to put his brother, Hank, on the major-league roster for the final month of the season—when every team can expand to 40 players—just so Hank could build up 30 more days towards his big-league pension. The remarkable thing is that Dick's talent was so apparent that he could command these concessions—even though, for a time, the Allens were more renowned for basketball than baseball. Three of his brothers had been all-state basketball players and he followed in their tradition. Though his high school in Wampum was one of the smallest in the state—it had only 30 boys—it built, in Dick's years, a string of 82 consecutive wins and won two state championships. He had scores of scholarship offers to college, but baseball offered a route out of poverty. So he took it.

He was still a kid at the time, a shy, hesitant country kid whose life was wrapped up in his family and in the family farm (where he first learned to love horses). In his first year in the minor leagues, he rolled up $400 in long-distance phone calls, just to talk with his mother and family. In his first three years in the minor leagues, he played in and around the Pennsylvania-New York environs which embraced "home." In his fourth year, he was sent—in one of those inexplicable, almost cruel decisions which so often mark management in baseball—to Little Rock, Arkansas. It was a town still torn by racial tensions—President Eisenhower had to send federal troops there in order to get black children admitted to the city's all-white high school—and Allen, barely 20 years old, was the first black baseball player to be assigned to Little Rock. "I felt different down there," he was to remember later. "It was as if I wasn't a human being. I couldn't go here and I couldn't go there ... I'll tell you what it was like: it was as if I was playing baseball in a prison. A fellow who does that loves playing baseball while he's at it, but he can't forget entirely that he's locked up." Nor could the locals let him forget: he was bombarded with crank phone calls and with signs that read, "Go home, nigger." If they meant to humiliate him, it didn't work. If they meant to frighten and disgust him, it did work. "There I am, looking around the stands and praying, 'Please God, don't let the ball be hit to me.' The pitcher cranks up and—whoosh!—a line drive right at me, no more than a foot over my head. I couldn't raise my arm. I couldn't even chase the ball. I was scared to death." For a while he thought about quitting and going home, but his mother told him he couldn't come home a quitter. So he hung in there and batted .297 and hit 33 home runs and by season's end was accepted as the "Most Popular Player" by the fans in Little Rock.

The next year, he was in the major leagues to stay. The 1964 Phillies had to find a place for him to play: he'd played in the outfield, at shortstop, second base and first base in the minor leagues—so the Phillies put him at third base. He was something of a butcher there—but he got better. And better. And better. And he won the Rookie of the Year award unanimously. The reason: his .318 batting average and his almost incredible power with the bat.

Allen is not a big man—5 feet 10 inches tall in the 187 pound range. Yet he hits with the power of a man who is 50 or 100 pounds of muscle bigger than he is. To be sure, much of the secret is in his wrists: he can cock the bat and snap it at the ball—in the last micro-second—like a man cracking a whip. The "wrist-hitter" had become a high fashion in baseball in the ten years before Allen arrived: Ernie Banks and Hank Aaron had ushered in the era of the "Slim Slugger." They also were wrist-hitters but they tended to use very-light bats: 30-31-32 ounces much of the time. What made Allen so singular is that he got the power of his chest, shoulder, and biceps into the blow—as well as his wrists—and he was swinging a 40-ounce bat while doing it. In short, his bats weigh a half-pound more than those of other sluggers his size. From his very first spring, the tales of his power surged through big-league baseball with each story more unbelievable—and more factual—than the last: he hit a fly ball that hit an obstruction some 100 feet high when the ball was 360 feet from home plate. Last season at White Sox park, he hit a ball that passed over a score board 50 feet high some 408 feet from home plate. Often he hit homers that were measured at 500 to 565 feet. "One of these days," said Gene Mauch, his first big-league manager, "I wouldn't be surprised if Richie homered to both left and right field at the same time. He'll split the ball in half with his strength."

But it was not to be in Philadelphia. The disappointment of that near-miss in 1964 hung on the fans—and they hung it on Allen. They remembered not his homers but his errors—he made 41 of them, more than any other third-baseman, in his rookie years. And his strikeouts: his

138 whiffs were a record. That was another record he'd break. The next year he got into a fight that was racial as well as personal with teammate Frank Thomas. It wound up with Thomas hitting him with a bat—and with Thomas, a favorite of the fans, being released by the club within hours. Thomas got his chance to go on television to explain his side of the story but Allen was forbidden by the ball club to reply, under the threat of a $1,500 fine. So Allen turned up as the mute villain in the incident. "When I showed my face the next night," he has recalled, "the fans booed and threw things and everything went downhill after that. Well, Willie Mays has had fights with guys. Hank Aaron and Rico Carty got in a fight in a plane and nobody said anything. Man, Gene Mauch actually called players into his office and invited them to rumble with him. Thousands of other ballplayers have had disagreements. But my thing went on for some six or seven years."

The more he was called a churl, the more he acted churlish. He wouldn't tip his hat after a homer. He wouldn't show up to play long-ball in batting practice. He wouldn't sign autographs. Everything he did became a cause célèbre: if he missed a plane, or came in late for a game, or had an accident pushing his car, it was because he was "trouble." And there was something "sinister" about his trouble: people in baseball and out began saying that he had "a drinking problem." There *were* times when he stayed out all night: once he threw a $1500 all-night party for his teammates and showed up, somewhat sleepstarved, at the ball park the next day in time to hit two homers off Tom Seaver of the New York Mets.

He is perfectly candid in acknowledging that he wasn't consuming soda pop at those parties. Or other times. "To be honest," he told Newsweek magazine last summer, "I was nervous under all that pressure and a couple of drinks would settle me down. The press would smell liquor on my breath and—bam!—I'm supposed to be drunk. But I never walked on the field where I couldn't do the job better than anybody else. Ain't nobody ever seen me stagger and fall around a ball field. No man, not even me, can hit two home runs in a game drunk."

Eventually, even the Phils recognized that he wasn't ever going to be as productive for them, as they'd hoped. So they traded him to St. Louis before the 1970 season.

He batted .279 there but he was among the league leaders in slugging (.560) and on reaching-base (.435).

By way of comparison, Johnny Bench on Cincinnati slugged at .587 and had an on-base percentage of .385— yet got 22 out of 24-first-place votes for the Most Valuable player in 1970. (But then Bench's team *did* win the pennant and Allen's team finished fourth in their division.) So he was traded again, this time to Los Angeles, and he batted .295 there. He virtually carried the team in a torrid pennant race with his hitting down the stretch, but LA and Allen—lost again, this time by a single game. So he was traded again—this time to the White Sox, for a left-handed pitcher with a losing record (13-16 in 1971) named Tommy John.

Walt Alston, manager of the Los Angeles Dodgers, took pains to deny there was any trouble with Allen. "The fact that he didn't take batting practice didn't bug me," he said. "I've managed in the big leagues for 18 years and I think that Allen's attitude towards batting practice is right. The batting practice we take now isn't much. The batters want half-speed pitches down the middle so they can try to knock the ball out of the park. But they don't get those kind of pitches in a game. For batting practice to mean anything, you should get curves and fast balls and certainly not know what is coming. I think that a player might need to loosen up but Allen has a good idea on batting practice not meaning too much.

"Now why did we trade Allen? Well, we had a wealth of outfielders. It looked to me like Allen's best position is first base but I had Wes Parker there. It boiled down to this: what will help us more, an extra first baseman or pitching help? So we traded Allen to the White Sox for Tommy John." And the Dodgers finished third in 1972, 10½ games out of first place.

In none of this was there any suggestion that Allen had talked back to his managers or his teammates. He is not rude or crude; he is no wild-eyed radical seeking fiery confrontations with The Establishment. He is, in fact, a rather quiet-spoken, even congenial individual who simply chooses to go his own way—in the conviction that his way is the best way. On the field, in ball games, he puts out 110 percent—he is never trying to be less than the best. But the problem is, as Maury Wills, his teammate at Los

Angeles, once pointed out, that "they want you to produce, but they want you to produce *their* way."

This is the core of what people call "the trouble with Dick Allen": he produces but he doesn't produce *their* way. He is, in fact, always testing-testing-testing—his way against the "baseball" way. He is matching his vision of life against the boss's. And this is escalated into another and more formidable contest: his ego vs. the owner's ... or the manager's. He is forcing them to accept him on his terms, not on theirs. And this is what so many men in baseball hold against him: that he's won—he's played better than they ever dreamed he could play (or they could play) by doing it his way. And there are many in baseball who hate him for it.

What Dick Allen has done is draw the line between the well-paid serfdom of big-league baseball—and being his own man. The one message he's delivered to baseball—to its owners, its managers, its fans, its writers—is that baseball can buy his talents as a player for money. But it can't buy him—as a man—for money.

This sense of independence angers bosses and astonishes players. There is a decided inclination in baseball—as in most other organizations: business, political, military— that "you go along to get along." Allen wouldn't do that: he'd get along on his own—and do it brilliantly. There were some who said it would disrupt a team to have to live with a genius who marched to a different drummer— himself. Yet it was not apparent on a team like the White Sox. Or even the Dodgers. "The disruption wasn't that great," said Maury Wills. "The players liked him. He's just one of those guys who can't go along with the group in everything. I think I'd try to find a way to live with it. It's the lesser of two evils." Willie Davis of the Dodgers noted that "there's something in his makeup that makes him fight certain things. I shudder to think of how great he could be if he could go at it like some other guys do, but he's pretty good the way he is."

The problem is not in his production but in the constant testing of egos. Almost every boss—owner or manager— tires of being tested and that's when Allen is shipped out. The gift of the White Sox is they accept him as he is—he tested and tested and tested them, and they never got uptight about it. He'd drift into spring training camp for a conversation, and then disappear without signing. He'd leave a phone number and they couldn't reach him at it. In fact, he didn't sign until training camp was all over; he began working out just after the players went on strike—as the baseball season was supposed to open. But he was ready when the strike was over and the season did open: he hit a home run in the first game of the season, he hit a double to break a tie in the next game or so, he made two spectacular fielding plays, and by the time the Sox came home from their first road trip, he was hitting .417. By All-Star time, he'd made so spectacular an impression all over the American League that he drew more votes than any other player in the league.

The significant thing is that he did as he always tried to do: on the one hand, he worked closely with his teammates—on opening day, he made a point of stopping and introducing himself to every player and wishing them the best of luck. He looked to players who were having troubles and went and talked with them, as best he could. He watched Bill Melton, the slugging third-baseman of the White Sox—who'd led the American League in home runs in 1971—trying to get untracked at the beginning of 1972. Melton had suffered a back injury while falling off a ladder in the off-season and now he was having trouble getting his big swing into the groove. Yet it was vital to the White Sox that he do it: with Allen, Melton, and Carlos May in the batting order, there'd be no way to pitch around one man to get at the other—they could demolish the pick-and-choose strategy if they could all hit almost as one. (May wound up with the same batting average as Allen, in fact—.308.) So one day in May, Melton got a phone call from Allen: "Hey, Billy, when you going to get out to the ballpark tonight?" Melton figured about same time as always—around 5 p.m. before a night game. "Let's you and me get out there a couple hours early and get in some extra batting practice," urged Allen. "We can't let them (the enemy pitchers) get at us." That day, Allen and Melton spent two extra hours taking batting practice and talking techniques of batting. Melton got a homer that night and so did Allen. Melton got a homer the next night and so did Allen. And the White Sox won both games.

At the same time, Allen was always testing his bosses. He was late for the team bus—it was the simplest and most direct test of Tanner. The manager held the bus patiently for 17 minutes until Allen showed up. ("C'mon, let's go ... he can catch a cab to the airport," grumbled one newsman. Tanner turned on him: "*You* can catch a cab to the airport," he snapped. "This *team* always goes together.") The denouement: Allen quietly developed a reputation for being the first-man-on-the-bus.

When Allen began skipping batting practice, Tanner carefully avoided making it an incident-for-confrontation. In fact, he told the whole team to skip batting practice (though he quickly changed his mind when the rest of the team went into a batting slump—while Allen didn't).

Tanner established his own test early in June when the Yankees were in Chicago for a Sunday doubleheader that drew 51,904 fans and left 8,000 milling outside the ballpark, unable to get in. It was the biggest White Sox crowd in 18 years and—for a team that had been counting fans in the pairs and trios, not by the thousands—it was a great thrill and rare opportunity. In such a situation, the fans want to see the Superstar—Dick Allen!—and it's *de rigueur* that the manager let him play. If he doesn't, he's got to answer not only to the fans but to the owner. This was the occasion when Tanner chose to let Allen—who does not like to exhaust himself in doubleheaders—sit out the second game on the bench. "He's played every inning this year," said Tanner, "and he deserves a rest." As soon as the lineups went up on the scoreboard—without Allen—Tanner got the expected phone call from the owner, John Allyn. "Where is Allen?" Tanner had an answer for him: "I'm saving him for late in the game. I'll send him in to pinch hit with a couple men on base so he can hit a homer and win the game for us." Tanner was as good as his word—and so was Allen: the Yanks had a 4-2 lead in the last of the ninth when the White Sox put two runners on base. Tanner turned to Allen: "Okay, Dick, go in and hit." Allen did—against the toughest pitcher the Yanks had to offer, Sparky Lyle. Allen took a strike, then a ball—and then rammed the next pitch 370 feet into the left-field grandstand ... to win the ball game, 5-4. And to climax a White Sox sweep of the Yankees.

The word got through to Allen: he was accepted in Chicago—and on his own terms. He showed his reaction in many ways other than his robust hitting: near the season's end, for example, he played doggedly through doubleheaders—no matter how tired he was—because the White Sox were still in the pennant race. And because Bill Melton had finally dropped out after a few weeks and seven homers with the herniated disc that sidelined him for the year. With Carlos May in a brief slump, there was no alternative for the White Sox to Allen and his slugging.

Dick expressed it verbally: "I'm more relaxed this year and I think I'm a little more outgoing."

And he expressed it temperamentally: he was able to make light of the somber reputation of the past. When he hit a homer after 9 o'clock one night, he was told by a newsman that he'd broken "curfew". Allen nodded: "I guess I've broken a few curfews in my time," he said.

Discovered by a newsman taking batting practice at 7 o'clock one morning, Allen told him the pitfalls of the practice: "If you write about it," he said with a laugh, "everybody will think I was just getting in."

In all of this, there was something in Dick Allen and his insight about the game that commanded respect. He had his goals for the team, not himself, and he didn't hesitate to express them: "If we can win 95 games, we'll take first place," he said. "Because 95 wins is going to be good enough to take this division." He was right: 95 wins would have given the White Sox a two-game bulge over Oakland—and thus made them the western division leader. Unfortunately, the White Sox didn't win 95 games; they won only 87 . . . and finished 5½ games behind Oakland.

So the season—with all its success—finished with less than complete fullfillment. And it was Dick Allen who delivered the epitaph on 1972—and the dawn of hope on 1973. "I've had everything from baseball, except the joy of playing on a winner," he said.

DICK ALLEN

Year	Club	Lea	Pos	AB	R	H	HR	RBI	Avg.
1960	Elmira	N.Y.-Pa.	SS	320	56	90	8	42	.281
1961	Twin Falls	Pioneer	2B	460	101	146	21	94	.317
1962	Williamsport	Eastern	OF-2B	511	97	168	20	109	.329
1963	Arkansas	Int.	OF	544	93	157	33	97	.289
1963	Philadelphia	N. L.	OF-3B	24	6	7	0	2	.292
1964	Philadelphia	N. L.	3B	632	125	201	29	91	.318
1965	Philadelphia	N. L.	3B-SS	619	93	187	20	85	.302
1966	Philadelphia	N. L.	3B-OF	524	112	166	40	110	.317
1967	Philadelphia	N. L.	3B-2B-SS	463	89	142	23	77	.307
1968	Philadelphia	N. L.	OF-3B	521	87	137	33	90	.263
1969	Philadelphia	N. L.	1B	438	79	126	32	89	.288
1970	St. Louis	N. L.	1B-3B-OF	459	88	128	34	101	.279
1971	Los Angeles	N. L.	3B-OF-1B	549	82	162	23	90	.295
1972	Chicago	A. L.	1B	506	90	156	37	113	.308

BILL FURLONG, a long-time contributor to Baseball Stars, is an outstanding free-lance writer from the Chicago area. His book on golfer Arnold Palmer entitled "Go For Broke" will be published this spring by Simon and Schuster.

JOHNNY BENCH

Oak Behind The Plate

by RAY ROBINSON

There are many ways to judge Johnny Bench, who is now the Most Valuable Player in the National League for the second time in the last three years.

You can look at his 1972 home run collection: 40, to lead the majors. His RBI's: 125, also to lead the majors. His splendid rifle-shot arm that intimidates enemy baserunners. His versatility—which enables him to catch or go to the outfield or to third base or first base, if his manager, Sparky Anderson, so decrees.

But the truest assessment of Johnny Bench probably springs from a memory of him from the ninth inning of the fifth game of the last World Series. There was one out. Cincinnati, behind in the Series, three games to one, held a 5-4 lead, but the Oakland A's were threatening. Blue Moon Odom, a pinch-runner, was perched on third base, eager to tie the score. Bert Campaneris, the Oakland shortstop, lifted a twisting foul fly not too far behind first base. The Reds' second baseman, Joe Morgan, made a good running catch on the wet grass, for the second out, then looked to see if Odom would dare to try for home and the tying run. Yes, Blue Moon had tagged up and set sail. Morgan steadied, slipped for an instant, recovered, then threw home to Bench, who stood guarding the plate—a baseball Rock of Gilbraltar—as the fleet Odom tried to beat the throw that was aimed at Bench's big catcher's glove.

And that's the Johnny Bench you have to judge. Odom did *not* score. The game was over. The Reds were still in the Series, down by just a game.

In situations like this one you don't try to win an edge on John Lee Bench, who may very well be the best ballplayer in the world today—and perhaps the greatest catcher the world has ever seen. At 24, he is already probably better than Bill Dickey of the old Yankees or Mickey Cochrane, who won fame with the Philadelphia Athletics and the Detroit Tigers or the ill-fated Roy Campanella of Brooklyn's "Boys of Summer" team.

"I'll tell you one thing," said manager Anderson, after Johnny had slapped the ball on the sliding Odom, "there's no way you're going to get through Johnny Bench if the game is close. He's absolutely the best in the business at blocking the plate."

So there is Johnny Bench, sturdier than a mighty oak, a power hitter who is the first catcher ever to lead either league in home runs. Yogi Berra, who hit more homers than any catcher in history, never did that; what's more, he never hit more than 30 HR's in any season. In less than six full seasons Bench has already led the National League in home runs twice. His 45 in 1970 paced the Reds to the flag that year.

Even if his performance in the '72 World Series hardly thrust him into a hero role, (as the Reds never seemed to recover from the hirsute rebellion conducted by the underdog Oaklands, in their green and gold get-ups), Bench was, none the less, fully appreciated by his rivals.

After the exciting seven-game set was over, Irv Noren, the Athletics' third base coach, joined so many others in giving unqualified endorsement to Johnny as the best catcher in the game. (Walter Alston, the venerable manager of the Los Angeles Dodgers, had already gone on record as saying that Bench will be "the All-Star catcher for the next ten years.")

"We heard a lot about Johnny before we ran into him in the Series," said Noren, who played with Yogi Berra on the Yanks, "but Johnny has to be seen to be believed. He has a fantastic arm, he's just like a cat around the plate, he hits the long ball and he has a great attitude. He's just about the most complete young player in baseball today."

Without Johnny Bench, of course, the Reds would never have landed in the World Series. It was his enormous ninth inning home run in the final playoff game against the Pittsburgh Pirates at Cincinnati, that tied up the ball game at 3-3, just when it appeared that all of his out-sized exertions of the regular season had come to naught.

To Larry Merchant, the sports columnist of the New York Post, that homer was "very great" because it was obvious, as Johnny batted against the Pirates' ace reliever, Dave Giusti, that he "was up there to hit one ... that's what Johnny Bench was supposed to do because that's what baseball is."

Midst the champagne merriment and semi-hysteria in the Cincinnati locker-room after the Reds went on from Johnny's HR to pull out the pennant, 4-3, on Bob Moose's wild pitch off home plate, Bench talked about that homer, his 41st of the year. "I felt so good today that I took a full swing at that pitch. I just knew I was going to hit it. Sometimes you just get that feeling. That's why I didn't concede my swing on a 1-2 count." As Dick Young of the New York Daily News was quick to point out, most good hitters protect the plate at such a point in a confrontation with a pitcher, especially when their team needs a run to tie. But Johnny wasn't up there protecting. "It was so dramatic," continued Bench. "When I touched home plate and looked over and saw the guys coming out of the dugout toward me, it was the greatest sight in the world. Their faces were so excited and they were smiling, from ear to ear. I really think it was the greatest moment of my life." Considering, too that Johnny already knew at that time that he'd have to go to the hospital after the season for lung surgery (an operation that was successful), his behavior was quite remarkable.

It's probably true to say that until 1971 Johnny had never really suffered any reversals to his general ambitions to become baseball's greatest catcher. Almost from the day he completed his minor league apprenticeship with Buffalo in 1967, where he crashed 23 home runs (one of every four hits he made was a HR), and was named Minor League Player of the Year, the arc of his progress was inexorably upward. The mark of the superplayer, the super-star was already upon him, and he was only barely out of his teens, and just a few miles removed from his home town in Binger (population 700), Oklahoma. Yogi Berra, having seen Johnny perform in the minors, said, without any hesitation, "He can do it all *now*."

And so Johnny did it all. He was confident, strong (six foot, 210 pounds), voluble, handsome and everybody's star of the future. In 1968, with 15 homers and a .275 average, he was proclaimed National League Rookie of the Year and the stories about how he could hold seven baseballs in one hand were spread quickly by an adoring press. In 1969 he hit 26 homers. And when pitchers on his own team watched him nail baserunners with throws that bee-lined just a few feet off the ground, they said, wistfully, that they would like to be able to throw the way Johnny Bench does.

It all led up to 1970, a year in which, at 22, Bench hit 45 home runs and drove home 148 runs, as he put together a .293 average. He was, indisputedly, the NL's Most Valuable Player, the leader of his club and a young man whose maturity in handling pitchers went unchallenged, even by those who were ten years his senior. In the World Series of 1970, though the Reds lost to the Baltimore Orioles, Johnny Bench spent his time turning Brooks Robinson into an acrobatic hero at third base. Everything he hit seemed to wind up in Robinson's vacuum cleaner glove at third. The baseball world applauded Brooks Robinson, while they said give Johnny Bench another ten years and he'll be better than Babe Ruth.

Then along came the 1971 season. And everything suddenly seemed to fall apart in the glittering world of the Oklahoma Kid. The hits stopped falling in, the homers stopped ringing off his big bat and the RBI's ceased. In short, it was a catastrophic season. A .238 average, 27 HR's, 61 RBI's (81 less than 1970). Nobody had thought that such ill luck would befall such a natural athlete, least of all Bench—and those who had pronounced Johnny as a sure Hall of Famer almost before he had reached voting age, were truly stunned by the letdown.

However, Joe Morgan, who had not been Johnny's teammate in the year of disaster, but had come over to the Reds from Houston in time for the 1972 season, volunteered an intelligent appraisal of the matter.

"The hangup with Johnny in 1971 was that he realized he might never have another year like 1970 again. He was," said Morgan, "a mature guy on the outside. But there's no way he could be mature on the inside at that age. He could communicate like a 28-year-old. But in his mind he suffered like a 23-year-old."

To Johnny Bench the year of failure was an embittering, but, perhaps, a sobering experience. "I tried to carry the team. But I couldn't," he says, "and I never could understand why."

The Reds had walked away with the National League pennant when Bench was operating the way Bench was supposed to operate; when he misfired in '71 the club seemed to fall apart at the seams and by the middle of August they were 15 games out of contention.

What made matters worse for Johnny was that prior to the 1971 season he had demanded a three-year contract for $500,000. He didn't get it. But his audacity in asking for it, didn't win him any friends in the Cincinnati front office or among many of his fans, who thought that that was chutzpah beyond recall. All this, before a man is 25 years old and hasn't proven himself beyond a shadow of doubt.

The fact is that Bench may have had an inferior year—for Johnny Bench—but the Reds didn't lose solely because he stopped being a run-making machine. There were other major factors for the Big Red Machine decline. Outfielder Bobby Tolan, a man who could get on base in front of Johnny, was out the whole year with a torn Achilles tendon and pitchers Wayne Simpson and Jim Merritt simply stopped winning ball games.

"In looking back," says Bench, "we took things for granted. You think things will always stay the same. But then they don't. So you try and you try and then you try too hard. Maybe we started out by being too complacent. Then when things started to get bad, there was frustration all around and it never got any better."

Determined to set things straight again in 1972, Bench geared himself emotionally and physically for a "comeback" at the age of 24. Then something happened that almost flipped him on his broad back. The first time Johnny came to bat on a full-house opening day at Cincinnati's Riverfront Stadium, the boos and catcalls rolled out of the stands.

"How soon they forget," said Chicago's third baseman Ron Santo, to the humiliated Bench.

"I had to think that everybody in the world heard those sounds," Bench later said.

Joe Morgan again put the matter in perspective. He told Steve Jacobson of Newsday, a Long Island newspaper, that "it's hard in a young mind to keep the boos from affecting you . . . when you're 23 or 24 you want cheers all the time. It's hard to say to a man like Bench that you've got to accept the bad with the good. He'd only had the good; now he was getting the bad. But now he understands better."

What Johnny Bench understood was that he had become a particularly vulnerable target because of all the publicity, the phenomenal year in 1971, his own supremely confident manner, his swollen salary. Maybe, too, he said, he was being put down by people, "those 8 to 5 working men," envious of Bench's working hours.

In retrospect, Bench feels that his 1971 year might have been a nasty interregnum for him, but possibly a valuable one, despite the indignities heaped on him by the fans. ("I don't believe," he said, "that anyone had ever been booed that bad before in Cincinnati.")

"Now I don't live and die with each game," he insists. "I've heard the boos and I've taken the jeers and I've had the cheers. I think the experience has helped me mature. After that 1971 year I'm sure there were plenty of people wondering whether my 1970 season was just a plain fluke. When you hear people turn on you the way they did on me in the beginning of the season, you have to wonder what it is they want of you. But I wanted to make 1972 a statisfying year."

When Johnny started out on the '72 campaign with only one hit in his first 22 times at bat, it didn't help to restore his confidence. But his bat started to connect shortly after that and in one early June spurt, he banged out seven homers in a five-game stretch, to tie a National League mark, set by Sunny Jim Bottomley in 1929.

By season's end, the boos, of course, had turned to acclamation. And maybe Bench has learned something from that turnaround, too. Maybe he knows now that the fans are as fickle as fate, and one has to live with both.

Ted Williams once autographed a baseball for Johnny. The slugger wrote: "To Johnny Bench, a Hall of Famer, for sure." And the Oakland "book" on Johnny that was gathered before the 1972 World Series suggested that if they had to start a southpaw against the Reds, it was highly advisable for him to "roll the ball to Bench."

Such encomiums are nice. They make good one-liners in newspaper stories and articles like this. But Bench knows now that a man can't rely on his press clippings, the esteem of his friends, his teammates or his parents. He still has to do it on the field—and not at Las Vegas or on the post-season banquet circuit.

"I want to be the greatest catcher ever to play this game," says Johnny Bench.

He probably will be—and 1972 may have been the critical time when it all turned around for him.

JOHNNY BENCH

Year	Club	Lea	Pos	AB	R	H	HR	RBI	Avg.
1965	Tampa	Fla.-St.	C-OF	214	29	53	2	35	.248
1966	Peninsula	Carolina	C	350	59	103	22	68	.294
1966	Buffalo	Int.	C	0	0	0	0	0	.000
1967	Buffalo	Int.	C-3B-OF-1B	344	39	89	23	68	.259
1967	Cincinnati	N. L.	C	86	7	14	1	6	.163
1968	Cincinnati	N. L.	C	564	67	155	15	82	.275
1969	Cincinnati	N. L.	C	532	83	156	26	90	.293
1970	Cincinnati	N. L.	C-OF-1B-3B	605	97	177	45	148	.293
1971	Cincinnati	N. L.	C-1B-OF-3B	562	80	134	27	61	.238
1972	Cincinnati	N. L.	C-1B	539	87	145	40	125	.269
World Series									
1970	Cincinnati	N. L.	C	19	3	4	1	3	.211
1972	Cincinnati	N. L.	C	23	4	6	1	1	.261

STEVE CARLTON

Super-Southpaw

by RAY ROBINSON

On a grey afternoon in Chicago's Wrigley Field last October, Steve Carlton hung up his 27th victory of the year. Under normal circumstances such left-handed achievement is noteworthy; even when Sandy Koufax won 27 games for the Los Angeles Dodgers in 1966 to set a modern record for lefthanders that was adjudged as a considerable feat, even though the Dodgers managed to win 68 other games that year, without the benefit of Sandy's services.

But, there is a convincing mathematical point about Steve Carlton's 1972 greatness, aside from the fact that it earned him, unanimously, the National League's Cy Young Award for pitchers. That Euclidean fact is that Koufax, by any measurement the finest southpaw of his time, won only a shade more than 28 percent of the Dodgers' total of wins (95) in 1966. Carlton, on the other hand, was responsible for an unheard of 45.8 percent of the Philadelphia Phillies' total of 59 victories in 1972, the most spectacular percentage in modern baseball history. If Steve had been "lucky" enough, for instance, to have pitched for the American League's Texas Rangers in '72, he would have wound up with exactly 50 percent of that team's wins, for the Rangers won only 54 times, low team on baseball's 24-club totem pole.

Carlton's productivity, in behalf of the third worst team in baseball—only Texas and San Diego won less games than the Phillies—earned him the nickname in Philadelphia of "The Franchise." Indeed, it wasn't more than a few days after the 1972 season closed that rumors began to circulate in the Hot Stove League that Steve would be traded for fully a quarter of the Pittsburgh Pirates' roster. General manager Paul Owens of the Phils didn't deny that there had been such rich offers. But he also made it quite clear that it would take a blockbuster of a proposal to pry super-southpaw Steve loose from his Philadelphia roots.

Such roots, of course, are now only a little over a year old. For it was only as recently as February 25, 1972, that Carlton made it to the clubhouse of the Phillies. He had spent some seven summers in the uniform of the St. Louis Cardinals, capped by his first 20-win season in the majors in 1971. As a reward for such services, the mustached Carlton, who has never sought to hide his somewhat maverick manners and attitudes from public view, went to Card owner Gussie Busch and asked for a sockful of money. Busch, perhaps painfully recalling that in 1970 Carlton had lost 19 games for St. Louis, disagreed with Steve's self-assessment. Within a few weeks, Busch's problem was solved and Steve's pride was assuaged: Carlton was traded off to the Phillies, in exchange for pitcher Rick Wise, a right-hander who had won 17 games for the Phils, including a no-hitter in 1971. When Wise went to the Philadelphia front office for a 100 percent raise over his '71 pay, the Phils decided, much as Busch did in St. Louis, that a change of scenery was in order. The Carlton-for-Wise swap was generally judged as a standoff, at the time it was made.

With Wise capturing only 16 games for the Cards in '72, while also losing 16, it looks more than ever that Mr. Busch should have stuck to his beer. In short, the curmudgeonly Busch was robbed! No amount of sophistry can persuade anyone today that Rick-for-Steve was an even-up deal—or close to it.

Certainly, nobody in Philadelphia, where the angry citizenry has been known to boo blind men and arthritic grandmothers, believes that. The churlish town that W. C. Fields defiled in his graveyard epitaph "Better to be here than in Philadelphia," practically turned out en masse for Steve every time he was scheduled to pitch at home, which was often. He was an automatic every-fourth day worker in '72 and credits such regularity for his success over the course of the season. Without Steve it's possible that the Phils wouldn't have come close to a million in attendance; the fans gave him more standing ovations last year than even the late Judy Garland ever earned in the old New York Palace.

On the way to the most satisfactory season anyone has had on a pitching rubber in Philadelphia since the early-1930s successes of the Athletics' Lefty Grove, Carlton led his league in practically everything, except cold showers. He had the most complete games, 30; most innings pitched, 346; most starts, 41; most wins, 27; most strikeouts, 310; and best earned run mark, 1.97. His eight shutouts were topped only by Dodger Don Sutton's nine.

And how did the tall (6' 4"), 195-pound Carlton, only the second National League pitcher in history (the other was Koufax) to strike out more than 300 batters in a season, react to his sudden eminence?

Well, for one thing, from the moment he joined the Phillies last spring he put himself on the record about one fact: "I'm going to win 20 again," he said. When the laughter subsided, he made everyone see that he had a perfectly serious face when he said it.

And how did he account for such unvarnished bragging? He had, he told reporters, altered his entire attitude about his occupation. The change had been wrought via the typewriter of a Tucson, Arizona night watchman. Without knowing Steve personally, the man had written him a series of admiring letters late in 1970—Steve's most disappointing campaign—stressing the value of "positive thinking." The first letter was 10 pages long.

"He wrote me," says Carlton, "that he was tired of seeing a guy with so much talent lose so much, and he said that he decided to write me after having a vision. Of course he couldn't have been more tired than I was of my losing . . .

"Those letters were beautiful stuff. He talked in depth about applying positive thinking. It changed my whole outlook on things. I have never written him. But he's the kind of person who forgives my ignorance . . ."

The result of all these admonitions? "I never even consider defeat now," insists Steve.

"Positive thinking" may have given Steve the mystic boost towards super-stardom in '72. But he happens to possess some other tools—just in case. Willie Stargell, the loose-swinging slugger of the Pittsburgh Pirates, once described what it's like to come up against Carlton. "It's like trying to drink coffee with a fork," he said.

The Carlton assets are a blazing fast ball that swooshes by batters with locomotive speed, a sharp-breaking curve that sportscasters sum up as "dipsy-doodling" and a slippery slider that has batters backing away, often in disbelief. All are delivered with an emphatic overhand propulsion and without typical pitcherly procrastination.

Only the sixth pitcher in the last 72 years to win over 20 games for a tail-end ball club, Steve supplements his highly visible repertoire with the competitive instincts of a marauding panther who has been deprived of food for a week. He has a fighting heart that would have endeared him to the late Vince Lombardi, the football coach who, it is said, believed that winning isn't everything—it's the only thing.

Though hurling for a team that has only a few respectable professionals on its roster—Carlton doesn't let it dampen his spirit or his unflagging desire to win. He's a winner among losers and refuses to be thrown off-stride by his teammates' incapacity to make runs for him. Ironically, in Carlton's 27th and final victory of the '72 season, the Phillies racked up eleven runs for him against the Chicago Cubs and, in the process, banged out six home runs, the most that had been hit by any team in the National League all year! Most of the time, however, the Phils provided him with little more than chicken-feed for support. That necessitated, of course, a policy of miserliness on Carlton's part. And he was wholly equal to the task.

In mid-summer, for instance, he put together a startling 15 wins in a row, losing finally to the Atlanta Braves, 2-1, in 11 innings, on August 21. An overflow crowd of 52,600 jammed Philadelphia's Veteran Memorial Stadium to see Steve try for his 16th in a row after a major traffic snarl held up the game for almost a half-hour. If the fans went away in disappointment, Steve managed to take it more philosophically.

"I just won't let myself get down if the team I'm pitching for doesn't manage to score many runs for me," said Carlton. "I try to encourage my hitters and that's all I can do. If we don't hit, then I just have to keep the other team from scoring. It's really as simple as that."

In one 63-inning stretch during his streak Carlton permitted just one earned run, as he went about hurling five shutouts and five one-run games. "I just can't believe anyone can pitch better than he has," said Phils' general manager Paul Owens. "He's some competitor!"

The "competitive" side of Carlton emerged, too, last June 25 in Montreal's Jarry Park. In the fourth inning, Ernie McAnally of the Montreal Expos hit Joe Lis of the Phillies with an errant pitch. In the bottom of the same inning, Carlton, who exhibited impeccable control in most of the National League-leading 346 innings he worked in '72 (he gave up 87 bases on balls and only twice all year did he yield two walks in a row), plunked Tim Foli of the Expos with a pitch. Without further ado, Gene Mauch, the Expos manager, raced from the Montreal dugout and aimed a prodigious right-hand punch at Carlton. Like most blows thrown in anger among ballplayers, this one failed to land on its target. Steve saw the thrust coming and managed to deflect it.

When a melee ensued, Mauch was tossed out of the game and things quieted down until Carlton came to bat in the top of the fifth inning. McAnally wound up and threw a ball precariously close to Steve's hip. Thereupon, the umps asked McAnally to leave the premises.

As a result of this brouhaha, all parties to the incident were fined—Mauch, McAnally, as well as Steve. The impost against Carlton was $50.

Later, when Steve was questioned about his role in the affair, he was, to say the least, more frank than most pitchers would have been under similar circumstances.

Insisting that Lis was hit intentionally, Carlton said "that's Mauch's type of baseball." What about his answer against the hot-headed Foli? "Yes, I threw at him," said Steve, in a rather astonishing admission. "But I didn't mean to hit him on the head. I simply retaliated. It's obvious that you have to retaliate in such a situation. I did. And I'm not ashamed of it."

One may not choose to commend Steve for his behavior. But rarely has a major league pitcher been quite that straightforward about his motivations.

After accomplishing so much with so little support in 1972, what does Steve Carlton look forward to in 1973?

For one, he'll need to put several more sensational years together before he really merits the comparisons that are now being made of himself to Sandy Koufax. Carlton appreciates this fact, for he has great admiration for Koufax and the record he compiled. "Any time you're linked with Sandy Koufax you're in good company—Sandy would have to be the best over a five-year period," he says. "But I'm not out chasing after somebody else's records—and not out chasing somebody else's reputation. All a guy can do is go out there and pitch each game the best he can. If the records fall, they fall. I just keep thinking about winning."

One thing Carlton can be assured of, as the 1973 season looms: he's the first $150,000 player in Phillies' history. And if he repeats his feats of 1972 in 1973—and if the Phillies are still as anemic as ever—he could very well surpass all the home run hitters and sluggers in the money department.

Could Super Steve be baseball's first $200,000 hurler? Tune in in 1973 to see how the soap opera is progressing!

RAY ROBINSON is the Editor of Seventeen *Magazine and the author of several popular books on baseball.*

STEVE CARLTON

Year	Club	Lea	IP	W	L	SO	BB	H	ERA
1964	Rock Hill	W. Carol.	79	10	1	91	36	39	1.03
1964	Winnipeg	Northern	75	4	4	79	48	63	3.36
1964	Tulsa	Texas	24	1	1	21	18	16	2.63
1965	St. Louis	N. L.	25	0	0	21	8	27	2.52
1966	Tulsa	P. C.	128	9	5	108	54	110	3.59
1966	St. Louis	N. L.	52	3	3	25	18	56	3.12
1967	St. Louis	N. L.	193	14	9	168	62	173	2.98
1968	St. Louis	N. L.	232	13	11	162	61	214	2.99
1969	St. Louis	N. L.	236	17	11	210	93	185	2.17
1970	St. Louis	N. L.	254	10	19	193	109	239	3.72
1971	St. Louis	N. L.	273	20	9	172	98	275	3.56
1972	Philadelphia	N. L.	346	27	10	310	87	256	1.97
World Series									
1967	St. Louis	N. L.	6	0	1	5	2	3	0.00
1968	St. Louis	N. L.	4	0	0	3	1	7	6.75

CESAR CEDENO

Hungry Hitter

by LARRY BORTSTEIN

Leo Durocher, manager of the Houston Astros, can credit an indulgent mother with helping to create his brightest young star.

Cesar Cedeno, who, at 22 years of age seems to possess unlimited potential for superstardom, grew up in Santo Domingo, Dominican Republic, where his parents ran a little store. After school young Cesar was expected to help his mother in the store, but invariably he would run off with his friends to play ball.

"Sometimes we wouldn't even go to school," grins Cesar sheepishly. "We'd just start out as if we were going there, then turn back and go to the baseball field. Most of the time I did go to school, though, and played ball when I was supposed to be in the store. My father didn't like baseball. When he caught me, he would whip me. He didn't want me to walk around town. He wanted me to keep busy. It was easy to get in trouble in those times."

What was the reaction of Cesar's mother to all this? "My mother, she was okay," Cesar says. "She bought me a new glove."

Cedeno's mother and, yes, even his father, must be proud of their offspring now that he has grown to manhood. In 1972, only his second full year in the major leagues, he exploded upon the rest of the National League with a roar.

Before his ouster late last season as manager of the Astros, Harry Walker, considered one of the finest judges of hitters in baseball, called Cesar "easily the best young hitter in the major leagues." The Dominican sensation, whose surname is pronounced Suh-DAYN-yo, was plastering National League pitching at a .350 clip at the time.

Through much of the season he was in contention for the batting championship, and as late as August 28 was atop the National League batting list with a robust .343 average—three points ahead of the Cubs' Billy Williams.

Williams eventually overtook Cesar—and so did Atlanta teammates Ralph Garr and Dusty Baker. But Cesar concluded the '72 campaign with a .320 average, a 56-point improvement over his .264 of 1971. For the second consecutive year, Cedeno topped the senior circuit in doubles. Driving them to all fields from his righthanded stance, the 6-2, 193-pounder belted 39 two-base hits in 1972, one fewer than the total with which he led the league in 1971.

Cedeno's average was up in 1972 and so were his home runs—way up. He clouted only eight out of the park in 1971, but nearly tripled that mark with 22 homers last season. "The extra weight he put on last year made him more of a power threat than we ever expected," observes Grady Hatton, a former Houston manager, now a coach for the Astros. "He could develop into a slugger."

If Cedeno does become an established home run hitter, he will break out of the mold that many baseball people cast for him only a couple years ago. Cesar has most often been compared to Roberto Clemente, the all-time great of the Pittsburgh Pirates, who reached the 3,000-hit plateau last season.

But Clemente, considerably smaller than Cedeno at 5-11, never has been a vaunted home run hitter, with a one-season high of 29 and only three years in which he belted more than 20 out of sight.

"We now feel Cesar has it in him to hit as many as 35 or 40 homers in a season," says the irrepressible Durocher, who took on the Astros' managership late last summer.

"When he's reached his full growth, Cesar should weigh about 210 or 215 pounds," says Durocher. "That will give him the strength to be a great power hitter. With all the other things he has going for him, he can't miss being the greatest player in the league for a long time." That sounds like Durocher sees Cedeno as a new Willie Mays. Willie always was Leo's favorite player, and anything resembling old No. 24 would go a long way toward easing the new career of a 66-year-old manager like Durocher.

Cedeno made a major stride last season in fulfilling Durocher's dream for him as the National League's top player. *The Sporting News*, baseball's bible, tapped Cesar second in the 1972 balloting for outstanding senior circuit performer, behind Billy Williams. In the Associated Press' nationwide election to determine the majors' all-star squad for 1972, Cesar was named the top centerfielder in baseball, and was named the middle man in an outfield alignment that also included Williams and Clemente.

Clemente acknowledges Cedeno's superstar credentials. "I think Cesar is the best player to come into the league since I've been playing," says Clemente. This is high praise indeed from a player not customarily given to laudatory comments about other major leaguers.

Hank Aaron, another National League batting star of some repute, puts it a little differently. When asked who was the last player as good as Cedeno to come into the league, the Atlanta Braves' immortal replies, "Me."

There is no phase of the game at which Cedeno is not adept. Base running? He stole 55 bases in 1972 to rank third in the National League behind Lou Brock, the perennial league-leader from St. Louis, and Joe Morgan, Cincinnati's little sparkplug. Cesar is exciting on the bases, running with his legs pumping rapidly in a piston-like fashion that indicates he might have been a fine running back or flanker in football, a game he never has played.

When Cedeno swings a bat, he uncoils and springs at a pitch and usually gets a piece of it. He struck out 104 times in 1971, decided that was "much too many," and swung in a more controlled arc last season. This resulted in greater long ball power and a greatly reduced whiff rate.

Defense? The mere fact that Cedeno plays center field, the toughest of the three outfield spots, indicates that he has excellent range and gets a good jump on a fly ball. He also has a fine throwing arm to complement his aggressive outfield play. In one game last summer the Cardinals' Joe Torre edged a little too far off first base on a line drive to center and Cedeno doubled him off the base with a perfect throw.

In the very next inning against St. Louis, Lou Brock was on first when a teammate grounded a single to center.

On most hits of this type, Brock is a virtual certainty to make it to third base. This time he made the turn around second, glanced at Cedeno, and held up.

It was Cesar's arm that originally earned him his chance for a career in baseball. He was a 16-year-old substitute first baseman and right fielder for a drug store team in his native Santo Domingo when a St. Louis Cardinal scout saw him throwing from the outfield before a game. The scout arranged for Cedeno to play with a local pro team for two weeks.

"I was scared," recalls Cesar. "But I hit .400. The Cardinals offered me $500 to sign, then $700, and then $1,000. After that, the scout had to go back to the States for a week and by the time he came back, Pat Gillick of the Astros had signed me for $3,000. The Cardinal scout came to my house about 15 minutes after I signed with the Astros, and he sure was mad!"

The scout who first eyed Cedeno for the Astros was John Mullen, who had just joined the Houston staff that spring of 1967. "John advised us to get a small bonus check ready," recalls Gillick, director of the club's eastern area scouts, "and Cesar took it. Now you couldn't get him for seven figures."

Gillick recalls that Diogene Cedeno, Cesar's father, was reluctant at first to grant permission to his son to sign a pro baseball contract. "We knew all about the way he had been against Cesar's playing baseball as a young boy," recalls Gillick. "His concern was that the boy was taking up too much time in an effort that would get him nothing. When we convinced the father that Cesar could make big money in baseball, he was impressed. He gave his permission right away. I'm not sure he understands yet just how great a player his son is going to become."

Perhaps no one yet has come close to gauging the extent of Cesar's talents. Harry Walker, who managed the Pirates before he piloted the Astros, attempted to place both Clemente and Cedeno in perspective last summer. "Cedeno is exciting everywhere," said Walker. "At bat, on the bases, and in the field. And perhaps the most exciting thing about him hasn't shown yet. I mean, speculation on how good he might be. Build his castles as high as you like and he might surpass them all.

"When I had Clemente at Pittsburgh," Walker continued, "he was the best. But Cesar could have a better record after four years than Roberto ever did."

When he was managing Houston, Walker used to talk to reporters for hours about Cedeno. Perhaps the most important point he made was this: "Cesar would make a mistake almost every day, but I didn't say a word to him. I didn't want to risk curbing his initiative, his desire. He knows when he's wrong and he corrects himself."

Cedeno classifies himself as a "hungry" hitter. "And I hope I always stay hungry," he says. "If I get three hits, I want four. If I steal one base, I want two. Being hungry makes playing baseball fun."

Fun for Cesar, perhaps, but not for the pitchers upon whom he has feasted in five professional leagues, including the National. With the Covington, Ky. club in the Appalachian League in 1968 Cedeno belted out hits at a .374 clip for 36 games and was elevated to Cocoa in the Florida State circuit late in the year. In 1969, then 18, Cesar spent the entire season with Peninsula in the Carolina League and batted .274 in fast company.

The Astros promoted Cedeno to their Oklahoma City farm in 1970, not quite convinced that the young Dominican could handle himself in the high minor league American Association. It took Cesar just 54 games to convince Houston club officials that he could indeed handle it. In fact, the American Association pitchers were happy to see the Astros elevate young Cedeno to the big club with just one-third of the 1970 campaign gone. Cesar was batting a cool .373 at the time.

In a 90-game major league effort in 1970, Cesar batted .310 though he was only 19. With the Astros building a solid, young club, manager Walker made Cedeno his regular centerfielder in 1971. It was not the season it could have been for Cesar or the Astros, though the second-year outfielder did drive in 81 runs and steal 20 bases. "Besides striking out too much, I got into a few slumps at the plate," recalls Cedeno, "and I wasn't able to get out of them. I would press more and more and the results would get worse.

"Last year," smiles Cesar, jumping ahead to his 1972 exploits, "I didn't have any real bad slump. At the beginning of the season I thought if I hit between .320 and .330 it would be a good season. I didn't want to brag about it to anybody, but I really thought I could do it, and I was glad that I did."

When asked about the batting title, Cesar shrugs and says, "I'll think about winning a batting title later. What I want most is to play in the World Series. If I do both in one year, that'll be tremendous. But the main thing is for us to win."

Before he left Houston, Harry Walker sounded what may be the future rallying cry for both Cedeno and the Astros. "Cesar plays as if he has rockets pushing him," said Walker. "And there's no stopping him now."

CESAR CEDENO

Year	Club	Lea	Pos	AB	R	H	HR	RBI	Avg.
1968	Covington _____ Appalachian		OF	131	23	49	0	21	.374
1968	Cocoa _____ Fla. St.		OF	180	19	46	0	16	.256
1969	Peninsula _____ Carolina		1B-OF	497	62	136	5	39	.274
1970	Oklahoma City _____ A. A.		OF	233	47	87	14	61	.373
1970	Houston _____ N. L.		OF	355	46	110	7	42	.310
1971	Houston _____ N. L.		OF-1B	611	85	161	10	81	.264
1972	Houston _____ N. L.		OF	559	104	179	22	82	.320

ROBERTO CLEMENTE

"Nobody Does Anything Better"

by RAY ROBINSON

EDITOR'S NOTE: Roberto Clemente, who was killed in a mission of mercy plane crash off Puerto Rico last New Year's Eve, as he attempted to fly to earthquake ravaged Nicaragua with relief supplies, may well have been the greatest ball player of his generation. The following article was retained in Baseball Stars of 1973 as one small final tribute to an indomitable man and athlete.

If baseball were full of Roberto Walker Clementes there wouldn't be a whisper abroad in the land that the game ever suffers a dull moment or that it is fighting decadence, dry rot or complacency.

For to Roberto Clemente, who has spent every summer since 1955 in the uniform of the Pittsburgh Pirates, each contest represents a grim personal challenge. His mere presence in a ball park is an incandescent moment for the game. An entire World Series—that of 1971—was dominated by his actions and personality. Long after people will have forgotten who the Pirates defeated in that Series—it was Baltimore—they will recall how Roberto Clemente hit, threw, fielded, hustled, ran and reacted under stress. Prior to that Series, it seems, most people had taken Clemente for granted, almost as if, by ignoring him, they were acknowledging his consistency and steady brilliance.

Clemente is baseball's home engagé (totally involved man). He is intense, proud, vibrantly alive and more dangerous than ever when wounded. For all of his 18 summers with the Pirates Roberto has been known somewhat lovingly, sometimes, deprecatingly, as Pittsburgh's "house hypochondriac." But, in truth, Clemente's so-called hypochondria has been a series of ailments that would have felled, if not discouraged, a lesser man.

He has made it through a veritable casebook of maladies, both mysterious and commonplace. There has always been a nagging pinched nerve in the neck, perhaps the most visible of all Roberto's physical bugaboos—how many times have fans watched him twisting his head in a gesture that is almost as characteristic for Roberto as the involuntary losing of his cap has been for Willie Mays? And there have been the tension headaches, the muscle spasms, the pulled muscles, the debilitating viruses, the heel injuries, the bone chips in his elbow, rheumatism in both ankles, spasms in the stomach, one leg that is supposed to be heavier than the other and an infection from the hogs on the San Juan farm he owns in Puerto Rico.

If you called Roberto Clemente this very moment he would probably tell you how hard it was this morning for him to tumble out of bed. A few years ago, after Roberto had raced around from first base to score on a single, he said, in all seriousness, as a footnote (no pun intended) to his daring, that "I had a sore foot. I wanted to rest it."

The dubious state of his health also enabled him to meet his wife. Nursing a bad leg, Clemente wandered into a drug store near San Juan to purchase some medicine. He got the medicine and also the sympathy of a beautiful young woman, who later arranged to marry Puerto Rico's greatest sports hero.

Over the years Clemente has openly resented the implication that he has ducked out of too many ball games due to his litany of ailments. Roberto feels he has been unduly penalized by the press and perhaps by some of his own teammates and fans, due to his frankness and outspokenness about the many ills that have plagued him.

During the 1971 World Series, Roberto said: "Nobody does anything better than me in baseball." He believed that, just as he believed in levelling with people about his physical condition and his predisposition to injuries. There is a lingering suspicion in Roberto's mind that he has been ridiculed all of these years about his health primarily because he is a Latin and Latins, in Roberto's baseball world, have never been accorded status as first-rate citizens and ballplayers.

"When Latin players say they are sick," Roberto said a few years ago, "people say it's all in the head."

Roberto has fought the suggestion of Latin inferiority every step of the way. Now, in what is the twilight of perhaps the most distinguished career of any Latin player, he seems finally to have won, for himself and others of Latin background, the kind of respect and admiration that has been long overdue them.

By no means was the summer of 1972 Roberto Clemente's finest hour. True, his average, which finished at .312, was not far removed from his lifetime batting mark of .318 (the highest of all active players). But Roberto came to plate only 378 times, which was an all-time low for his major league life. At the age of 38, Clemente could not force his besieged body to do the same things it had done in previous springs and summers.

Despite the relative letdown in overall productivity, Roberto still hit ten home runs and batted in 60 runs. In the five-game playoff to settle the National League flag, Clemente was hardly the one-man gang he'd been when he stole the show at the '71 World Series. Yet baseball's "fabulous invalid" stood out grimly in the fourth game of the playoff set against Cincinnati. While his team floundered in a game that was lost to the Reds, 7-1, Roberto managed to get the only two hits garnered by the Pirates off Ross Grimsley, the 21-year-old southpaw. The only run, as a matter of fact, that the Pirates, reputed to be the toughest batting order in baseball, got, was Clemente's lonely seventh inning home run.

However, there were signs of a diminution of Roberto's vitality in the first two playoff games. (Clemente has always been a remarkable performer in post-season games. He has never failed to get a hit in any of the 14 World Series games he's played in. He participated in seven games in the 1960 win over the Yankees and in seven against the Orioles in the '71 classic). But in those two opening playoff contests last year, before worshipful home town audiences in Pittsburgh, Clemente was stopped cold. Then, slightly revivified, as the Bucs moved to Cincinnati, Clemente went one-for-three, two-for-four and, in the final 4-3 defeat to Cincy, one-for-three.

Yet, it is unfair to deduce from this rather lackluster

(for him) performance, that Clemente is through, or even close to it. This is hardly a toothless, bent, withered old man in a wheel chair, as Los Angeles sport columnist Jim Murray reminds us. "His body still looks like something quarried by Michelangelo," Murray writes, "and he could throw a deer out at first base!"

Tony Kubek, the Game-of-the-Week broadcaster for NBC, also thinks it's entirely too early to be chiseling out Clemente's obituary. "He's remarkable," says Tony. "You can't lope to first base on a right field single with Roberto out there. He's apt to catch you napping at first with one of those patented throws of his—or at least he'll try."

So, if there were some lugubrious times in 1972 for Roberto, he still came on strong at some key moments. For example, on the night of June 19, playing before 15,400 Pittsburgh fans, he banged a two-run home run in the eighth inning, as the Pirates walloped the Los Angeles Dodgers, 13-3. It wasn't a clutch home run, by any means. But, in one respect, it was of signal importance for Roberto and it won him sustained applause from his fans. The blast shattered third baseman Pie Traynor's all-time Pittsburgh club record of 1,273 runs batted in.

Oddly enough, after breaking Pie's mark, Clemente did not emerge from the Buc dugouts to acknowledge the cheers that greeted his feat. Why didn't Roberto come out? Was he pulling a Ted Williams?

Roberto's answer to this question revealed what a sensitive and thoughtful human being he is. "The man who held the record," said Clemente, "just died. Out of my respect for him, I didn't want to tip my hat."

There aren't many professional athletes around who'd react that way to such a situation. Then Roberto added another thought about such mundane things as records.

"I don't like to worry about records and the record books," he said. "I've got a house full of trophies. But the thing that stands out to me is to be able to play to the best of my ability all the time."

Manager Bill Virdon, a modest man who succeeded Danny Murtaugh at the start of 1972 as the Pirates' skipper, expressed, at the time, his appreciation for his formidable employee.

"I don't think there's a 37-year-old around who can do the things Roberto can do on a ball field. To me, he's just impossible."

Topping the Pie Traynor mark was just another record, as far as Clemente was concerned. But the "big one" for Clemente in 1972 was gaining entry into baseball's rather exclusive 3,000-hit club. Among baseball's actives, only Hank Aaron and Willie Mays belong to this fraternity, while there are plenty of Hall of Famers, including Babe Ruth, Lou Gehrig, Jimmy Foxx, Bill Terry and Al Simmons who never rapped out 3,000 hits. Aside from Aaron and Mays, only eight other men, headed by Ty Cobb, Stan Musial and Tris Speaker, have made it into this hitting pantheon.

On the afternoon of September 30, Clemente joined these celebrated gentlemen. This time he stood out on second base, where he was perched as a result of his historic two-base hit, and raised his cap in a gesture of appreciation to the 13,000 fans who applauded him warmly. The hit was a booming double off Pittsburgh's left-center field wall off the delivery of the Mets' first-year hurler, Jon Matlack.

Umpire Doug Harvey retrieved the ball from the Mets' Jim Fregosi and handed it to Roberto as a precious souvenir. For several minutes the game came to a halt, as the crowd roared and Clemente soaked up the good will of the customers. When Roberto left the game in the next inning—presumably to "rest up for the playoffs"—elder statesman Willie Mays of the Mets trotted over from the New York dugout to compliment Roberto, as the cameras duly recorded the event for posterity.

Later, Roberto practiced the traditional ritual of identifying the pitch he had hit. "It was a curve ball," he said, "the same pitch he struck me out on in the first inning."

However, to make the occasion even more dramatic, Roberto insisted that he had spent a rather sleepless night, fielding phone calls from Puerto Rico and New York following the near-miss "3000th hit" that he *didn't* get in the game of Sept. 29. Clemente had, typically, lunged hard at an outside pitch and the ball leaked softly to Mets' second baseman Ken Boswell. When Boswell permitted the ball to skip off his glove, Roberto arrived safely at first base. It was one of those plays that Clemente might have beaten, even if Ken had fielded the ball cleanly. So the fans waited expectantly to see how the official scorer would document the time at bat—hit or error?

The scorer did react immediately. It was an error for

Boswell, in his judgment. But that message was not relayed properly to the scoreboard and the "H" sign, indicating base-hit, blinked its notice to the fans, who proceeded to celebrate, as it turned out, somewhat prematurely. When the correction was made, the big "E" for error, flashed on the scoreboard, the crowd booed its lungs out, as Clemente's blood pressure charged up the sphygmomanometer.

In three more plate appearances in the same game, Roberto didn't come close to another hit off Tom Seaver. After the game, Roberto, still seething about the E call, engaged in his own peculiar brand of "popping-off."

"Did you really want to take that squibbler for your 3000th hit?" asked a reporter.

"Why not?" answered Roberto, a man to whom base hits have been the very blood of his life. "A hit's a hit."

When Clemente was told that Ken Boswell thought it was an error and that he would have thrown Clemente out had he fielded the ball cleanly, Roberto snorted, "Boswell's full of it."

But Clemente refused to put a period to the discussion at that point. "I knew it was a hit," he continued. "Everybody knew it was a hit. The umpire said it was a hit. But I'm used to this sort of thing. Anyway I'm glad they didn't call it a hit. This shows what they've been doing to me for 18 years."

An angry, rash statement, perhaps, with the usual touch of martyrdom. But how far from the truth? When a man becomes a super-star, and Clemente has been that in baseball for many years, sometimes the breaks and calls come his way. But before his certification for canonization, did Clemente suffer any prejudiced treatment from official scorers? There is no record kept anywhere of such exotic matters. But was there a smidgen of truth to what Roberto Clemente was saying?

The next afternoon, Roberto Clemente showed up to play—and to hit—and he got his 3000th hit, as everyone knew he would.

But with all of the honors, the stellar World Series performances, the picture book plays that he has been making every year of his big league career, Clemente is not yet convinced that people appreciate his true dimensions as a diamond hero.

"People do not think of me as a great player," he insists.

"The writers do not write about me as a great player. So if I don't boast about myself, nobody does. Writers are always surprised when Clemente makes a great play. But I make the great play all the time."

Roberto Clemente is right—and he is also wrong.

Anyone who is not blind knows how great he is.

ROBERTO CLEMENTE

Year	Club	Lea	Pos	AB	R	H	HR	RBI	Avg.
1954	Montreal	Int.	OF-3B	148	27	38	2	12	.257
1955	Pittsburgh	N. L.	OF	474	48	121	5	47	.255
1956	Pittsburgh	N. L.	OF-2B-3B	543	66	169	7	60	.311
1957	Pittsburgh	N. L.	OF	451	42	114	4	30	.253
1958	Pittsburgh	N. L.	OF	519	69	150	6	50	.289
1959	Pittsburgh	N. L.	OF	432	60	128	4	50	.296
1960	Pittsburgh	N. L.	OF	570	89	179	16	94	.314
1961	Pittsburgh	N. L.	OF	572	100	201	23	89	.351
1962	Pittsburgh	N. L.	OF	538	95	168	10	74	.312
1963	Pittsburgh	N. L.	OF	600	77	192	17	76	.320
1964	Pittsburgh	N. L.	OF	622	95	211	12	87	.339
1965	Pittsburgh	N. L.	OF	589	91	194	10	65	.329
1966	Pittsburgh	N. L.	OF	638	105	202	29	119	.317
1967	Pittsburgh	N. L.	OF	585	103	209	23	110	.357
1968	Pittsburgh	N. L.	OF	502	74	146	18	57	.291
1969	Pittsburgh	N. L.	OF	507	87	175	19	91	.345
1970	Pittsburgh	N. L.	OF	412	65	145	14	60	.352
1971	Pittsburgh	N. L.	OF	522	82	178	13	86	.341
1972	Pittsburgh	N. L.	OF	378	68	118	10	60	.312
	World Series								
1960	Pittsburgh	N. L.	OF	29	1	9	0	3	.310
1971	Pittsburgh	N. L.	OF	29	3	12	2	4	.414

NATE COLBERT

The "Wild" Day

by LARRY BORTSTEIN

On May 2, 1954, at St. Louis' old Busch Stadium, Stan Musial of the Cardinals had one of the greatest slugging days in baseball history. He blasted five home runs in a doubleheader against the New York Giants.

One of those watching "The Man's" extraordinary achievement in wide-eyed wonderment from the stands was a young lad, just turned eight, who idolized Musial, as did most St. Louis youngsters of the period. "I recall that day very well," said the boy many years later, when he was a grown man. "It was a Sunday and as I watched Stan hit one homer after another, I couldn't believe anyone could ever do something like that again."

The man was recalling that long-ago afternoon in St. Louis one day last summer for a very special reason. Musial's record had gone unchallenged for more than 18 years until a hot night in August, 1972. Then the boy from St. Louis, all grown up, wearing the baseball uniform of the San Diego Padres, a team that hadn't even existed in the National League 18 years earlier, matched Musial's doubleheader achievement, homer for homer.

The boy-turned-man was, of course, Nathan Colbert, Jr., whose night of devastation in Atlanta last August 1 was called by ex-Braves' manager Lum Harris, "the greatest night any player's ever had."

Colbert's one-man explosion powered the Padres to a sweep of the twilight-night twin bill against Atlanta, 9-0, in the opener, when he smacked two homers and two singles, and drove in five runs, and 11-7 in the nightcap, when he drove in eight runs with three homers, one a grand slam.

The display enabled San Diego's first baseman to establish a new record for RBI's during a doubleheader. His 13 RBI's erased the mark of 11 shared by three American Leaguers—Cleveland's Earl Averill in 1930, Boston's Jim Tabor in 1939, and Baltimore's Boog Powell in 1966. Nate also cracked the National League mark of 10, established by Enos Slaughter of the Cardinals in 1947. Colbert's 22 total bases also broke Musial's doubleheader mark of 21, set the day he whacked his five homers.

Colbert arrived in Atlanta with an ailing knee that he'd injured while sliding home with a run the previous week. But Nate had decided he wasn't going to ask to be taken out of the lineup. "I was going to get in there no matter how I felt," he recalls, "because I wanted to play in that Atlanta park. Any fly ball hit there has a chance of going out." The Braves' home park annually produces more baseballs flying out of it than any other in the National League.

Before the twin bill, Padre coach Whitey Wietelmann suggested that Nate might be able to reach the friendly seats a couple times that night. "After I hit the fourth one," Colbert recalled later, "I looked over at Whitey and he was cracking up. I said to myself, 'this is something wild'," the 26-year-old slugger added.

It appeared that Nate never would get a chance to try for his fifth homer of the night when Cecil Upshaw, one of a long succession of Braves' hurlers, quickly retired the first two San Diego batters in the ninth inning of the second game. Colbert went to the on-deck circle as Larry Stahl stepped to the plate for the Padres. If Upshaw retired Stahl, Nate wouldn't get another chance to bat.

But Stahl punched a seeing-eye single just out of the reach of Larvell Blanks, the second baseman, and Nate stepped to the plate to face the sidearmer "who always gave me trouble."

Colbert smacked Upshaw's first offering, a high, inside fast ball, over the left field fence, drawing a standing ovation from a few thousand Braves' fans who had remained to the end. It was Nate's fifth home run off five different Atlanta pitchers.

Rounding second base, Colbert told the umpire, "I don't

believe this." The umpire, Bruce Froemming, replied, "I don't believe it, either."

Hank Aaron believed it. Playing on the receiving side of the slugging this particular evening, Aaron, the greatest right-handed hitting home run slugger in history, said, "The thing that really was impressive about Colbert's performance was that he hit the five homers to different fields. Three went to left field, one went to center, and one went to right, and none of them was cheap. He didn't even swing hard. That's what I've always believed myself—that you don't have to swing hard to hit a home run. I see Colbert believes in that, too."

Many observers around the senior circuit believe in Nate Colbert, even though he has suffered a severe lack of publicity because he plays for a team that never has finished out of last place in its four years of existence. "The lack of publicity doesn't bother me," Colbert says. "Naturally, I'd like to see us win more games and do better in the standings, but the Padres have taken very good care of me financially, especially considering our attendance which hasn't been too good. I don't care all that much about being fussed over, and it's not because I don't like people."

The people who most "fuss over" Nate are the rival managers who must devise ways for their pitchers to work against the 6-2, 210-pounder. "I used to think Lee May was the strongest hitter in the league," says Sparky Anderson of Cincinnati, "but now I think Nate is. He's strong enough to get no more than a piece of the ball and still drive it out of the park. And he's awfully hard to fool."

Gene Mauch of Montreal also extols Colbert's virtues. "He can really bomb you," says the Expos' field boss. "Make a mistake and the ball's gone."

Because of the puny Padre attack, opposing teams have concentrated their efforts on pitching to Nate when they face San Diego. He never has hit for a high average, with a .264 mark in 1971 his personal one-year peak. In 1972 he batted .250, a modest mark, but there was nothing modest about the rest of his statistics. He hit 38 home runs, ranking second in the major leagues only to National League Most Valuable Player Johnny Bench. Colbert had a previous 38-homer season, 1970. But his 111 runs batted in during 1972 represented his first time over the century mark and was fourth best in the National League. The only NL sluggers ahead of Nate in 1972 RBI's were Bench, Billy Williams, and Willie Stargell.

Nearly one-half of Colbert's hits in 1972 went for extra bases. In addition to his 38 roundtrippers he also included 27 doubles and two triples in his 141 hits.

In his first four full seasons in the majors, 1969-72, Nate socked 127 baseballs out of the park, a pace of almost 32 homers per season. Only two recently active players in the majors did better in the home run department their first four years than did Colbert. They were Willie Mays, who powered 148 homers over the span, and Frank Robinson, who hit 134. Mays' first four full seasons in the majors covered six years, because he missed the 1952 and 1953 campaigns in military service.

By contrast, Johnny Bench totaled 113 homers his first four big-league seasons, Willie McCovey managed 100, Hank Aaron, 110, and Willie Stargell, 92.

Cincinnati manager Anderson is not surprised at Colbert's accomplishments. "When I coached for the Padres in 1969," recalls Anderson, "the guys used to tease him and call him Claudette, because of the actress' name Claudette Colbert. But he shut them up the way he could hit the ball. I thought then that Nate could some day hit 50 homers in one year. Now I believe I was being conservative. If he played in Atlanta, or Chicago, Philadelphia, or Montreal, where the fences are relatively short and the winds blow, he'd have a great chance to break the one-season record for homers."

Nate was one of the players selected by the Padres in 1969 when they were stocking personnel for their first year as an expansion team in the NL. He had been selected off the Houston list of eligible draftees. Colbert had been the property of the Astros since 1965, when he joined their Midwest League farm club in Cedar Rapids, Iowa.

In 1966 Nate received a brief look from the Astros, but got to bat only seven times, during which he went hitless. After belting 28 homers for Amarillo in the Texas League in 1967, Colbert was again summoned to Houston in 1968, but after delivering only eight hits in 53 trips, and only one extra base hit, a double, he was sent to Oklahoma City in the Pacific Coast League. Nate's 8-for-60 batting performance in his two tries with Houston didn't induce the Astros to protect him when the draft to stock the expansion San Diego and Montreal franchises was conducted during the 1968 offseason.

"I didn't like the idea of being taken by an expansion team," confesses Colbert. "But Houston seemed to be set at first base. At least they were using lots of different guys ahead of me, and I didn't think I'd ever get another chance to stick with them."

Nate had no trouble gaining the regular first-base job for the Padres in their infant season, and he was just about the club's only bright spot that 1969 campaign. He hit 24 homers and batted in 66 runs to lead the club in both power categories. He delighted what few Padre supporters there were with an aggressive style at the plate. He struck out more times than San Diego management would have liked—123—but regularly connected safely on bad pitches. "I don't pay too much attention to the strike zone," Nate shrugs. "Any pitch I can reach with the bat I figure is a good pitch to hit. That's why I don't get many walks."

While Nate's free tickets to first base aren't frequent, his strikeouts have been, though they have dropped gradually the past couple seasons. Colbert's whiff peak was 150 in 1970, but he fanned only 119 times the next season.

"I tell him not to worry about striking out," says Padre skipper Don Zimmer. "I tell him to take good cuts, not to stand around up there. That's what he likes to do, and that's what we like him to do.

"I think Nate really started coming into his own last year when he took off about 25 pounds before he came to spring training," adds Zimmer. "Last year he was bringing the bat around faster than he ever had before. He was more dangerous a hitter. I think he'll be even more dangerous as he goes along."

Though Colbert zoomed into national prominence when he unleashed his five-homer barrage in the doubleheader against Atlanta last August 1, he already had enjoyed some memorable highlights in his big-league career. For example, on the next to last day of the 1971 season, he clubbed a three-run homer off San Francisco relief pitcher Jerry Johnson to give San Diego a 10-inning, 4-1 victory, and send the NL pennant race between the Giants and Los Angeles Dodgers down to the last day. San Francisco clinched the Western Division flag the next day, but

Colbert's blow off Johnson caused the Giants considerable anxiety.

The week before he pole-axed the Braves last season, Nate scored the winning run for the National League in the All-Star Game, also at Atlanta. This was another 10-inning affair. Colbert, the lone San Diego representative in the midstream classic for the second straight year, pinch-hit for New York relief pitcher Tug McGraw and led off the bottom of the 10th with a walk. He moved to second on a sacrifice by Giant shortstop Chris Speier.

"I was standing on second and thinking about a collision at the plate, so I could get in the All-Star re-runs like Pete Rose," Nate recalls. Rose was the hero of the 1970 All-Star Game when he knocked Cleveland catcher Ray Fosse out cold in a home-plate collision to score the winning run. "I was staring at Carlton Fisk (the American League receiver) and sizing him up. I figured I could take him."

Colbert's study of the opposing catcher proved unnecessary. Joe Morgan drove a Dave McNally pitch into right center and Nate scored the winning run with ease.

Though he would have preferred barreling into home plate in more heroic manner, Colbert was comforted by the thought that it was his run that won for the National League. "It's nice to be considered an All-Star," he said. "After all, this league has maybe the best players in baseball. It's good to be one of them."

Harry Walker, who was managing at Houston when Nate had his tryouts there, feels that the San Diego first-sacker has become a "truly professional hitter. You can usually look at any hitter and find something he's doing wrong or some area where he might improve," says Walker, one of the best analysts of the art of hitting. "But you look at Colbert and you say to yourself, 'He's got it all. He does everything right.'"

NATE COLBERT

Year	Club	Lea	Pos	AB	R	H	HR	RBI	Avg.
1964	Sarasota Cards	Sar. Rk.	1B-OF	83	20	18	2	13	.217
1965	Cedar Rapids	Midwest	1B	285	46	78	9	45	.274
1966	Houston	N. L.	PH	7	3	0	0	0	.000
1967	Oklahoma City	P. C.	OF	5	0	0	0	0	.000
1967	Amarillo	Texas	OF-1B-3B	434	82	127	28	67	.293
1968	Oklahoma City	P. C.	OF-1B-3B	322	52	85	14	44	.264
1968	Houston	N. L.	OF-1B	53	5	8	0	4	.151
1969	San Diego	N. L.	1B	483	64	123	24	66	.255
1970	San Diego	N. L.	1B-3B	572	84	148	38	86	.259
1971	San Diego	N. L.	1B	565	81	149	27	84	.264
1972	San Diego	N. L.	1B	563	87	141	38	111	.250

DICK ALLEN—
Chicago White Sox

NOLAN RYAN—
California Angels

PRINTED IN U.S.A.

STEVE CARLTON—
Philadelphia Phillies

CESAR CEDENO—
Houston Astros

WILBUR WOOD—
Chicago White Sox

LUIS TIANT—
Boston Red Sox

PETE ROSE—Cincinnati Reds

GENE TENACE—
Oakland Athletics

The late
ROBERTO CLEMENTE—
Pittsburgh Pirates

JOHNNY BENCH—
Cincinnati Reds

CARLTON FISK—
Boston Red Sox

NATE COLBERT—
San Diego Padres

BILLY WILLIAMS—
Chicago Cubs

HANK AARON—
Atlanta Braves

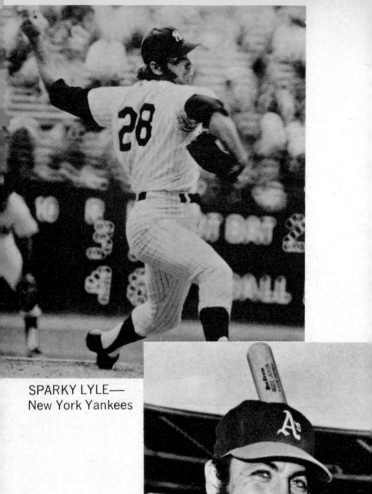

SPARKY LYLE—
New York Yankees

MIKE EPSTEIN—
Texas Rangers

LARRY BORTSTEIN writes about all sports, but his first love is baseball. He still carries on an affair with the game, a romance which his wife knows about and, in fact, encourages.

MIKE EPSTEIN

Vulnerable Guy

by ARNOLD HANO

There is something vulnerable about Mike Epstein. He's big, 6-4, 211 pounds. He's strong. He's intelligent, articulate, a man with a sense of who he is, what he wants, where he's going. He's got a gorgeous wife, two adorable daughters, a house in the hills, a job he loves.

Yet withal, vulnerable.

Consider. It is the World Series. Some pitcher on the Reds, it doesn't matter which one, they all were the same to Epstein, 0-for-16, has thrown a strike, and Epstein has either taken it, badly fooled, or he's swung and missed, badly fooled. Epstein steps out, and stares into space, a man deep in his thoughts. He strokes his mustache, he muses, he seems to shake his head. It is almost as if he expects what will now transpire. He steps back in, and strikes out, or grounds out feebly, or softly pops up. They have taken his bat away, and without it, Mike Epstein is nothing. A very vulnerable man.

Consider further. It is the second game of the World Series. Oakland has won the first, and is leading in the second by one run. Epstein walks in the sixth inning, and manager Dick Williams immediately jerks him off the basepaths and puts in a pinch-runner. The A's potentially biggest bat is throttled for the remainder of the game. Epstein blows up at Williams on the plane back to Oakland. Williams blows back in kind, a man who doesn't like to have his decisions questioned, even when dead sober. But Epstein doesn't like to be benched. He sulks. "He's a moody player," somebody once said of Epstein.

"And I'm a moody manager," Williams shot back. "And I'm a moody owner," Charles O. Finley tossed in.

The message is clear. Don't rock the boat. Don't make waves. Mike Epstein likes to rock, likes to ripple. Dick Williams likes to pull men out of the lineup, puppets on his string. And Charles O. Finley likes to deal off players on a whim. The Mike Epsteins are the meat of baseball to the Dick Williamses and Charles O. Finleys, beef to be sold by the pound. Vulnerable. (In early December, 1972, in a trade that raised more than a few eyebrows, the "vulnerable" Epstein was marketed away by Finley. Mike went to the lowly Texas Rangers for relief hurler Horacio Pina, who had a 2-7 record in 1972.)

Perhaps Mike Epstein never should have played professional baseball. Intellectuals have a difficult time, in baseball. Intellectuals play professional football, professional basketball. Intellectuals even box, or own boxers. The intellectuals who manage to get into baseball—the Jim Boutons and Jim Brosnans—often end up miserable, frustrated, vulnerable individuals. Baseball poses undue hardships to the thinking man. The game itself may be an unwinding poem to the knowing spectator. But to the player it is scattered verses, broken rhymes, one time at bat every two or three innings, one play in the field every 10 or 15 pitches. You fill endless space and time on the baseball field, constantly frustrated by a game that often leaves you out, innings at a stretch. When Mike Epstein played with Baltimore, and nobody wanted him, he spent most of his time on the bench and fairly ached to be traded. "I can't let this parade pass me by," he said, in his urgent metaphorical speech, which makes him something of a Clifford Odets phrasemaker of the ball field. Then he got traded to Washington, and he played more regularly, but still the parade passed him by. Stardom beckoned, superstardom even, and he was teased by dreams of glory, until their lack of fulfillment drove him up the wall. Manager Ted Williams, who insisted all of his players be made in his image (and knew they could not) benched Epstein against left-handed pitching. Epstein loathed the inactivity, yes, but he loathed the humiliation more. He is a man who must prove himself, over and over, a man in a squirrel cage, driving himself and getting nowhere.

"I'd talk to the manager all day," he said. "It hurts. It

puts your back against the wall. You can't go anywhere. I felt I was wasting my time. I had a chance to make money if I proved myself. No player is content to make $40,000 when you can make $100,000." If he proved himself.

So he got traded again, to Oakland, and he played more regularly, and still the parade passed him by. He hit a ton for Oakland in 1971 when he first joined the team. Darold Knowles, who came over to Oakland from Washington with Epstein, said, "I think he's concentrating a lot more than he did." Dick Williams said, "Mike's always been a bear-down-son-of-a-gun." Epstein sopped it all up. "You take more pride with a first-place club."

Then, inexplicably, he stopped hitting. Like that. Epstein today thinks it was because he got too involved in the family's new house, in the Oakland hills. He painted this and built that and fixed the other. He missed his mid-day nap. He wore himself out. Or so he thinks, now. He ended up having a miserable season. Williams benched him for the 1971 playoffs against Baltimore. Epstein almost quit baseball after 1971. "I'd let a lot of people down," he said. "Things had snowballed."

Even before the 1971 slump, he had his miseries. He'd been hitting that ton, when the A's bought Orlando Cepeda from Atlanta. "Great," Epstein thought at first. "Big bat." But the players began talking how Williams would platoon the two first basemen, sitting Epstein down against lefthanders. Mike, whose ego cannot take this sort of rejection, went up to manager Williams. He yelled, "I break my butt for you, and this is what I get," and Williams yelled back "If I've got to baby a player to keep him happy, I might as well get out of the game." And Williams knew *he* wasn't going to get out of the game. Which leaves guess-who vulnerable?

Remember that conversation, concerning Cepeda. It is, almost word for word, the World Series dialogue that transpired in the sky, between Cincinnati and Oakland, after Williams had removed Epstein in the second game for a runner. One man cried out how he'd busted his butt, and the other man said, Sure you did, that's what I expect from my players.

Enough of this. Mike Epstein had put together a fine year, one of the best he's ever had. He hit .270, 23 points better than his lifetime average. He flogged 26 home runs.

Only two men in his league, Dick Allen and Bobby Murcer, hit more. He knocked in 70 runs. Had he not missed nine games in late July and early August because of an eye infection, and other games before and after, he would have hit 30 home runs and knocked in 80-plus runs. Even without the ifs, a good year. He once had a better year, in 1969 at Washington, when he slugged out 30 home runs. He'll never hit for a high average. He is a free swinger who strikes out a lot. He is a line drive hitter who has to be exactly right in his timing. He must play regularly, or he loses that fine-edged reflex.

So, despite the good year, he was more vulnerable than ever. In that last game of the Series, you may have seen the Oakland club of the future. Gene Tenace played first base, with Mike Hegan in reserve. Dave Duncan caught. Mike Epstein sat in the dugout, stroking his mustache. Less than two months later Mike was gone from that dugout and from Oakland. Epstein is at his peak, but the downhill days may come quickly, as he reaches 30 years old this April. Epstein once ran the 100 in 10.2. Now they take him out for runners. Epstein has painfully lifted himself from defensive mediocrity in the field to a bare adequacy. Mike Hegan is a superb fielder. Gene Tenace, with his versatility, gets the job done. Tenace's slugging feats in the Series may presage a hitting career that could help allay the possible loss of Epstein's bat. And remember, Mike Hegan hit .329 in his infrequent appearances in 1972.

Mike Epstein's always been vulnerable, odd man out. He is a Jew in what is basically a gentile sport. He is an egghead, in a hard-hat sport. He is a rugged individual in a world of organization men. He reads and spouts Emerson on Self-Reliance and Simplicity. He practices Thoreau and Teddy Roosevelt. He is a disciple of the individualism of writer Ayn Rand. He likes to sleep out on the deck of his Oakland house, so he can be close to the browsing deer. He builds rifles and cartridges, and he takes to the woods every winter, in the subzero cold of Wyoming. Where other players drive bigger and fancier cars every year, Epstein drives a Ford truck, the only car his family owns. And Epstein meditates. He turns on the record player and he closes his eyes. "I take off an hour each day like that. I lie on my bed, the music turned up, and I look at the scene. I come to peace with myself."

Life is a series of coming to peaces for Mike Epstein. It guards him against going to pieces. Life is also a series of proofs. Why did Mike Epstein choose to play baseball? "I had to prove I could compete in the big leagues. I couldn't go through life not knowing if I could have done it. I would have eaten my heart out every time I saw a box score, if I hadn't tried."

When he attended the University of California at Berkeley, he tried out for the football team. Three fullbacks were ahead of him, upperclassmen. Sophomore Epstein had to beat them out. He did. He became the varsity fullback in his first game.

He met Barbara Gluskin in Stockton, California, where Mike played minor league ball, after college. Barbara had a beau. Epstein had to beat him out. He did. They married in 1966. He went to Baltimore, in 1967, where Boog Powell had a lock on first base, so Epstein had no chance to prove himself. So he made the usual, "Play me or trade me," ultimatum. Baltimore, as usual, ignored it. So Epstein quit. Actually quit. "I figured I was wasting time. I could go out on my own. Life wasn't worth it." He went home for three weeks. Baltimore traded him.

He went to Washington, where Ted Williams entered his life in 1969, and Mike Epstein polished his hitting. But no hitter, especially a big left-handed hitter, can satisfy Ted Williams, so Epstein rode the bench, a platoon player, and that humiliates a man who must prove himself. "It was discouraging," Epstein said. "In another line of work, if you don't get a chance to prove yourself, you can go to another company. Not in baseball."

So he asked to be traded again, and they sent him to Oakland. You know the rest.

Where does he go from here? Once he threatened to be a big star. Once he appeared on the verge of becoming the best first baseman in his league. Maybe for a spell he was. Now there is Dick Allen and young John Mayberry. On single days, Epstein is still one of the best, and maybe the best. Like the time he hit three home runs in one game, May 16, 1969. The day he knocked in eight runs against Baltimore, in 1970. The two days in 1971 when he hit four home runs in four consecutive at-bats, to tie a record.

But on the overall, he remains where he is, between journeyman and superstar, a new member of manager

Whitey Herzog's cast in Arlington, Texas. "I've never met Epstein in my life," says Ranger pilot Herzog. "But I hope he does the same job for us as he did for Oakland."

Epstein is torn by the Oakland experience, where he helped bring a world's championship to the Bay area. But he was humiliated by his performance in that world championship competition. He will say of himself, "You can't polish dirt," minutes after he says, "Everything germinates in the mind. You can think yourself into a slump. You can make yourself into a winning player."

Perhaps the two are not irreconcilable. You *can* make yourself into a winning player, but will you? The ideal yields to the pragmatic. And Mike Epstein, at 30, faces an uncertain future. He is a proud man. "Everything I own," he says, "I owe to one thing. My own hands. It's a wonderful feeling. Nobody ever gave me a gift. When I'm finished with baseball, I want to be able to say, 'This is the best Mike Epstein could do. I did the best my ability could take me.'"

Yet he knows his ability could take him farther than it has. He wonders why superstardom is barely out of reach. Perhaps in 1973 the goal and the reality will merge. It's going to have to happen soon, or not at all. And this time, in Texas.

MIKE EPSTEIN

Year	Club	Lea	Pos	AB	R	H	HR	RBI	Avg.
1965	Stockton	Calif.	1B	399	83	135	30	100	.338
1966	Rochester	Int.	1B	473	79	146	29	102	.309
1966	Baltimore	A. L.	1B	11	1	2	0	3	.182
1967	Balt.-Washington	A. L.	1B	297	32	67	9	29	.226
1968	Buffalo	Int.	1B	35	9	14	5	13	.400
1968	Washington	A. L.	1B	385	40	90	13	33	.234
1969	Washington	A. L.	1B	403	73	112	30	85	.278
1970	Washington	A. L.	1B	430	55	110	20	56	.256
1971	Wash.-Oakland	A. L.	1B	414	49	98	19	60	.237
1972	Oakland	A. L.	1B	455	63	122	26	70	.268
	World Series								
1972	Oakland	A. L.	1B	16	1	0	0	0	.000

CARLTON FISK

Take-Charge Backstop

by AL HIRSHBERG

The unexpected surge of the Red Sox in the 1972 American League East race was almost the direct result of casual criticism of his elders by Carlton (Pudge) Fisk, a remarkably talented rookie catcher. Since the Red Sox haven't had such a multi-skilled catcher of any age or experience since Birdie Tebbetts's time, Fisk's very presence in the lineup had a beneficial effect. Beyond that, the 24-year-old youth from New Hampshire inspired the whole team by publicly proclaiming—without meaning to—that the Red Sox weren't getting the leadership they needed from their veteran stars, Carl Yastrzemski and Reggie Smith.

Actually, Fisk's remarks were less proclamation than accident. When he made them to a Springfield, Mass., sports writer, he thought he was talking off the record. He soon found out the difference between off the record and off the cuff, for Boston papers picked up the story and plastered it all over their front pages.

It looked like another case of dissension in the ranks. This is an occupational hazard with all Red Sox teams, who never seem to be able to stand prosperity. For some reason or other, cliques form, bickering begins, and the upshot usually is a bitter exchange among the noble athletes themselves.

This time it didn't work out that way. All the players seemed to get along fine, especially with Fisk. Neither a knocker nor a grudge-holder, the young man who started the season as the club's third-string catcher and was its No. 1 man within two weeks had a well-earned reputation of being a nice guy who wouldn't put the slug on his worst enemy.

Instead of splitting the team into rival camps, his remarks to the Springfield scribe closed the ranks. From the day of Fisk's indiscretion on, the Red Sox were hot contenders for their division championship. For more reasons than one, the man responsible was Pudge Fisk.

However, his off-the-field comments were nothing compared to his on-the-field achievements. A fiery, smart, tireless receiver, Fisk was the season's outstanding rookie and, after Bill Freehan of the Tigers was hurt, the American League's outstanding catcher. The only rookie in the All-Star game, he ended the year eighth among the league's top hitters, at .293, and was at or near the leadership of his club in nearly every offensive category.

He disproved the popular notion (based largely on fact) that catchers are the truck-horses on their feet by stealing five bases and sharing the leadership of the league with Joe Rudi of the A's in triples. Both had nine. His 22 home runs were the most ever hit by a Red Sox catcher. He won 11 games with clutch hits, seven of them homers. He helped develop two fine rookie pitchers, John Curtis and Lynn McGlothen and gave badly-needed confidence to Luis Tiant, the Cuban hurler who made the comeback of the year.

Fisk was the best all-round hitter the Red Sox had. He led the team in batting average, home runs and triples. He was second in hits and doubles, third in games played and runs, and fourth in runs batted in. And, after lamenting the club's lack of leadership, he himself took over. On the field, he was the boss, not only of the pitchers, but everyone else.

A slump in the final week of the season was all that kept Fisk from hitting .300. He was at or near that figure all season. That was a big surprise, since he had never come close in a full minor league campaign. But if his 1972 performance is any criterion, he has a good chance of becoming a consistent .300 hitter.

Perhaps most surprising of all was how the Red Sox overlooked him. Always in search of a catcher of big league caliber (they once dropped over half a million dollars down the bonus drain for young receivers) they went to Winter Haven, Fla., in the spring of 1972 with three possibilities. The most experienced was Duane

Josephson, obtained in a trade with the White Sox. Next in line was Bob Montgomery, who seemed ticketed for the job if Josephson wouldn't do.

Last on the list was Pudge Fisk. In four minor league seasons, he hadn't made a dent. His only real credentials were a pair of homers when the Red Sox brought him up from their Louisville farm club at the end of the 1971 season. Even those belts into Fenway Park's chummy left field screen didn't seem to mean much.

But Fisk is a right-handed batter with power and the ability to pull the ball. Any good right-handed pull hitter is a thing of beauty and a joy forever in Boston. It is only 315 feet from the plate to the left field fence down the foul line, and the fence breaks out towards center so gradually that it has always been a popular target for right-handers.

At 6-foot-2 and 200 pounds, the baby-faced Fisk is hardly a runt, yet he seemed a long way from rating as a regular when he reported to manager Eddie Kasko in the spring. There was just too much traffic ahead of him. In order to make it off the bench, he had to get by both Josephson and Montgomery.

While he failed to do it in spring training, it came surprisingly easy to him once the season began. At that point Josephson was number one, but the former White Sox receiver was hurt the day after the season began, following the players' strike. Montgomery moved in and Fisk moved up a notch on the bench.

Two days after Montgomery's debut, Fisk got his chance, and took full advantage of it. Besides showing all kinds of nerve and life and ability behind the plate, he beat the Yankees with a triple. From then on, he was home, catching 131 of the 155 Red Sox games and starring in many of them.

Although his home has always been the tiny town of Charlestown, New Hampshire, Fisk has close identification with Vermont. Charlestown, which is right on the state line, is so small it has few schools and neither industrial, medical nor organized sports facilities of its own. Pudge was born in a Bellows Falls, Vermont, hospital, went to Bellows Falls High School and played American Legion ball in Bellows Falls. His father is a machinist, working in Springfield, Vt.

Thus Vermont, with good reason, staked a claim to him

when he made it so big in the American League, and Fisk accepts the fact that he owes much of his success to his opportunities there. He was an all-Vermont schoolboy basketball player, and until he moved into professional baseball, basketball was his favorite sport. He once scored 40 points and had 32 rebounds in one game, and later entered the University of New Hampshire on a basketball scholarship.

But he was also a most promising baseball player, pitching and playing shortstop as well as catching. At 15, he hit a 500-foot home run at Bellows Falls, a sock still unofficially recognized as the longest ever hit by anyone in the State of Vermont. And in 1965 Fisk was named Vermont's American Legion baseball player-of-the-year.

His coach, Bert Stewart, was a Red Sox bird dog who worked closely with Jack Burns, long-time Red Sox scout in the New England area. It was Stewart who recommended Fisk to Burns, who then signed the youth to a Red Sox contract in 1967 after Pudge's sophomore year in college. Fisk was 19 years old at the time.

"I think I waited too long," Fisk says today. "I should have started at 17 instead of going to college. Maybe I would have reached the majors sooner."

This was no rap at college in general, for Fisk continued his education even after going into organized baseball. And, since he has always intended to get a college education, Fisk is sure he would have started seeking one even if he had signed a baseball contract at 17. He transferred from New Hampshire to Keene Teachers College after signing with the Red Sox.

Because of military commitments, he didn't play ball anywhere his first year in the Red Sox system. A year later, the same commitments kept down his minor league play to 62 games at Waterloo in the Midwest League. Not until 1969, when he moved to Pittsfield in the Eastern League did he play a full season. There, he batted only .242, but hit ten homers and drove in 41 runs. He spent the whole 1970 season at Pawtucket, another Eastern League club, where he did so poorly he nearly retired. Even 12 homers and 44 RBI's couldn't compensate for a .229 batting average.

His wife, whom he met in college, talked him into playing one more year. At Louisville, the top Red Sox farm club, he had his best minor league season despite a shoulder separation that kept him out of about a third of the International League games. But he hit .263, had 10 homers and 43 RBI's and, for the first time, really attracted the attention of the Red Sox brass with his catching.

Possessor of one of the best arms in baseball, Fisk is now the nearest thing to Johnny Bench in the American League. He is no easier to run on than Bench, and he has the same type of take-charge attitude that has made the Reds' star the top catcher in baseball. There is also every reason to believe that Fisk, now that his feet are really wet in big league competition, will sooner or later be able to hit with Bench.

Manager Earl Weaver of the Orioles, who managed the American Leaguers in the 1972 All-Star game, personally chose Fisk as his number two catcher behind Bill Freehan. Actually, that was how Fisk's own peers voted him. While only fifth in the fans' popularity contest (since his name wasn't on the ballot, all his votes had to be write-ins), Fisk was second in the poll of American League ballplayers.

He caught the last five innings of the game against the National League at Atlanta, and it was hardly his fault that the Americans lost in extra innings. In the eighth Fisk got a hit and scored the tying run. During the time he caught, he handled Gaylord Perry of the Indians, Wilbur Wood of the White Sox and Dave McNally of the Orioles.

One of Fisk's greatest assets is his supreme self-confidence. Unlike other catchers, who use a special glove to catch Wood's knuckler for example, Fisk used a regulation sized glove and had neither errors or passed balls in the two innings Wood worked. Asked how he managed, he said, "If your reflexes are fast enough you can do it by waiting on the knuckler until the last second."

Few ballplayers, catchers or otherwise, have reflexes as fast as Fisk's. He can move so quickly that he once engineered a rare double play when the Orioles tried a suicide squeeze one night at Fenway Park. An almost impossible play to stop if the ball is bunted fair, Fisk broke it up by pushing the batter aside, pouncing on the ball while it was still moving and tagging the runner coming in, before throwing to first for the double play.

He has an uncanny ability to catch pop fouls. A few springs ago, when he first went to Winter Haven with the

Red Sox, he exhausted Dick Williams, then the manager, who hit fungo pops to his catchers one day to see who would last the longest. When Fisk was the sole survivor Williams said, "I'll keep hitting them until you drop one."

"That suits me," Fisk said. "But you might be hitting them all day."

"He never did drop one," Williams said later. "I figured then that this kid was sure to make it some day."

The day has arrived.

CARLTON FISK

Year	Club	Lea	Pos	AB	R	H	HR	RBI	Avg.
1967	Greenville	W. Carolinas			(In Military Service)				
1968	Waterloo	Midwest	C	195	31	66	12	34	.338
1969	Pittsfield	Eastern	C	309	38	75	10	41	.243
1969	Boston	A. L.	C	5	0	0	0	0	.000
1970	Pawtucket	Eastern	C-OF	284	43	65	12	44	.229
1971	Louisville	Int.	C-OF-3B	308	45	81	10	43	.263
1971	Boston	A. L.	C	48	7	15	2	6	.313
1972	Boston	A. L.	C	457	74	134	22	61	.293

SPARKY LYLE

Late-Inning Magic

by ROBERT G. DEINDORFER

Back before the world was out of joint, back when we were all of us younger and more innocent, way back then, the swaggering pin-striped New York Yankees dominated big league baseball by constantly producing muscular heroes whose epic feats have since passed into folklore.

In the wistful eye of memory we can see them still, strong men swinging thunderous bats, Babe Ruth, Lou Gehrig and Bill Dickey, Joe DiMaggio, Mickey Mantle and Yogi Berra. So many other stars—Joe Gordon, Red Ruffing, Tony Lazzeri, Allie Reynolds, Phil Rizzuto, Whitey Ford, Elston Howard, Bobby Richardson, Clete Boyer, Hank Bauer—crowded the grassy flats of Yankee Stadium that not all of them got their rightful due. In annual All-Star games the American League even took to strengthening its team by naming such Yank spare parts as Gene Woodling, Joe Page and Johnny Mize.

If a number of those Yankee heroes amounted to genuine celebrities, bigger than baseball, almost bigger than life, well, perhaps they were that, too. When Babe Ruth missed a few games due to a stomach ache, or when one of Mickey Mantle's fragile knees came apart or when Roger Maris seriously started to close in on the asterisk home run record, newspapers pulled the stories out of the parochial sports section and bannered them on page one.

But nothing—not even the championship star-spangled Yanks—can last forever. All of a sudden the San Francisco wharves, the Oklahoma lead mines and a Baltimore orphanage weren't producing superstars any more, not for the Yankees, anyway. As the team fell to as low as last place and attendance figures fizzled, management tried to pump up players like Roy White, Mel Stottlemyre and the promising Bobby Murcer into full-blown heroes, without quite fooling anyone.

Into these woeful circumstances, enter Albert W. (Sparky) Lyle, a breezy left-handed relief pitcher with a big chaw of Red Man tobacco in one cheek and a sense of mental calm so great he could have slept through thunderous World War Two. More than anyone else, it was Lyle who not only lifted the faded Yanks into the boiling American League East pennant race for a few suspenseful weeks last summer but also brought them surging back to the respectability missing for all too many seasons.

Day after day, the six-foot, 200-pounder held precarious leads the Yanks scratched together. He literally attacked rival hitters with a basic fast ball and an oily slider. His impact couldn't possibly have been greater. After Lyle contributed to eight out of nine victories in mid-August, for example, manager Ralph Houk decided to rest him for a few days. The club promptly went out and lost four in a row.

Final inventory figures for 1972 show that other AL relief pitchers will be shooting at his marks for a long time to come. In running up a new league record of 35 saves, the aggressive southpaw struck out 75 hitters, while allowing only 85 hits in 108 innings of showdown crisis pitching. More impressive still, his 35 saves accounted for almost half the Yanks' 79 victories, which explains why Houk acts like a man who's just inherited a box of genuine Cuban cigars.

"Has this team got a certain magic?" a writer asked Houk as the pennant race tightened up.

"It has," Houk said. "Lyle is the magic."

But Sparky Lyle's contributions go beyond mere numbers, impressive as the numbers happen to be. It's the form as well as the substance that finally gives the Yanks what they've been searching for, a star in the grand old tradition, cocky, colorful, commanding, something to start fans to dreaming pennants, pennants, victories, victories. The fact that he's also mildly eccentric—Lyle enjoys squashing freshly-baked cakes that friends of teammates send to the clubhouse by sitting on the cakes, fully clothed—makes him all the more valuable in what has become a machine-made, by-the-numbers age of baseball conformity.

The vision of Lyle stalking out to the mound is enough to give even the most malevolent opposing hitters serious pause. With the Yankee Stadium organist playing "Pomp and Circumstance," he hops out of the curb service Datsun that fetches him in from the bullpen, strides angrily to the mound, fires four or five warmup pitches, glares balefully at the batter. In a typical appearance against Milwaukee last season, one-run lead, two men on base, nobody out, ninth inning, he put out the fire with exactly six pitches.

Despite the crisis situation and the rolling crowd noise, whether pro or con, any time Lyle arrives for his rescue act, he resists the pressure simply by ignoring it. Occasionally he isn't even aware of the identity of the man swinging a load of wood at the plate. In Houk's opinion, he has the ideal temperament for a reliever.

Personally, Lyle doesn't quarrel with that view.

Hear him.

"I don't listen to the crowd and I don't worry about who's up," he says. "No matter who it is I know I'm going to throw inside to right-handers and outside to left-handers. So I just concentrate on psyching myself up to attack them, to put them on the defensive."

"Even when I don't work, I stay ready." Lyle slouched on a seat in the clubhouse. "I'm always ready to pitch, right up to the final out. I never go to the bullpen with the idea that I hope I don't go in today. After all, relief pitching is 90 per cent mental—and I make sure I'm up for every game."

In an especially memorable game against Texas last summer, Lyle demonstrated exactly what he means by being "up." At the time he relieved Stottlemyre in the eighth inning, with the Yanks ahead, 3-2, Texas had runners on second and third with nobody out. Lyle positioned the chaw of Red Man in his left cheek, hurried five warmup pitches, two of them fast balls, three sliders and intentionally walked Frank Howard to load the bases, still with nobody out.

A flicker of despair ran through the grandstand. Obviously even the league's greatest reliever couldn't escape without at least a run scoring, because even a fly ball would cash in the runner on third. Lyle hitched at his pants, struck out Dick Billings, Larry Bittner and Ken Suarez—all three of them on just ten pitches.

Detroit manager Billy Martin, for one, a pragmatic man not given to sentimental gushes, blinks his tough guy eyes any time the conversation turns to Lyle, as it frequently does in dugouts around the league.

"Lyle should win something this year," he told a sportswriter last fall. "It would be a great thing for all relief pitchers if he got the Cy Young Award. It would give them the recognition they all deserve." (Lyle did *not* win it.)

In many ways, an informal comment by Yank pitcher Fritz Peterson's five-year-old son Gregg amounts to an even more emphatic tribute. After a home game in September a visitor asked Gregg to name the best team in the American League.

"Sparky Lyle," he promptly replied.

Gregg Peterson is no fool. Only an hour before, Lyle had pitched three scoreless innings to bail his old man out, for the seventh time, in a 3-2 victory over Boston.

Whether Houk and the front office are willing to admit it or not, Lyle has bailed them out some too. After a series of disastrous trades—Roger Maris for Charlie Smith, Clete Boyer for Bill Robinson, Stan Bahnsen for Rich McKinney—Houk swapped journeyman first baseman Danny Carter to Boston for Lyle in 1971.

"He could handle both left and right-handed hitters, which is most important for a reliever," Houk said, after admitting he'd been trying to land the durable southpaw for two years. "He's a real throwback to the oldtime ballplayers."

Maybe so. While his record with the Red Sox was fairly impressive—since first reaching the majors as a relief pitcher in 1967 Lyle saved 63 games—he didn't exactly strike anyone as a candidate for superstardom.

Even back home in smalltown DuBois, Pennsylvania Lyle hadn't shown much until he caught on with a sandlot team his junior year in high school. Using a slow curve and a very live fastball he struck out 31 hitters in a 17-inning game the day a Baltimore scout happened to stop by, which is why he became an Oriole farmhand briefly, before Boston drafted him.

In Sparky Lyle the team that Babe Ruth built gained a hero but lost the last of an old tradition. Modest hitters like Gene Michael, Horace Clarke, Roy White, Thurman

Munson, along with consistent long-ball Bobby Murcer, scratch for a few runs. Given a lead and seven or eight innings of good pitching by Peterson, Stottlemyre, Mike Kekich or Rob Gardner, Houk then is able to reach out to his bullpen for Lyle in an effort to lock up the game.

"Dee-fence ... dee-fence," fans chant fervently, as Lyle appears. And that's just what they get from the strapping left-hander—"Dee-fence"—and plenty of it.

In one key series with Detroit in mid-August, Lyle twice entered games at the start of the ninth to preserve one-run leads. He received credit for a third victory in relief of Peterson. All Lyle did in that stunning sweep was strike out seven batters and allow no runs in five innings. "Dee-fence."

With Lyle the hub to hold a short-winded pitching staff together, Yankee fans can't be blamed for spinning dreams of glory now that a promising new season is ahead. After all, the team has other bright spots in third baseman Graig Nettles, obtained from Cleveland and perhaps even Ron Blomberg who show signs of hitting with the brute power management has been yearning for for two years.

As for Houk himself, he still savors the memory of that record-breaking 35th save against Cleveland in September. In the ninth inning the Indians racked Gardner for a single and double, which was all Houk had been waiting for. In came Lyle to retire three straight hitters, two on strikeouts, and save the game.

Two weeks later, in an informal ceremony between games of a Sunday double-header, the Yanks showed that they know how to treat a brand new hero. Cocky Sparky Lyle was given the little Datsun that had been lugging him in from the bullpen all last season.

As a cynical old writer up in the press box observed, the car must have had 20,000 miles on it by then.

SPARKY LYLE

Year	Club	Lea	IP	W	L	SO	BB	H	ERA
1964	Bluefield	Appal.	33	3	2	44	25	23	4.36
1964	Fox Cities	Midwest	35	3	1	51	18	30	2.31
1965	Winston-Salem	Carolina	87	5	5	79	55	84	4.24
1966	Pittsfield	Eastern	74	4	2	72	43	62	3.65
1967	Toronto	Int.	21	2	2	17	14	13	1.71
1967	Boston	A. L.	43	1	2	42	14	33	2.30
1968	Boston	A. L.	66	6	1	52	14	67	2.73
1969	Boston	A. L.	103	8	3	93	48	91	2.53
1970	Boston	A. L.	67	1	7	51	37	62	3.90
1971	Boston	A. L.	52	6	4	37	23	41	2.77
1972	New York	A. L.	107	9	5	75	29	84	1.92

BOB DEINDORFER is an American, a Democrat, a Midwesterner and a Yankee fan—not necessarily in that order. He has contributed to Baseball Stars for more than fifteen years—and has also covered the sports scene for any number of national magazines.

PETE ROSE

The Hustlin' Man

by DAN SCHLOSSBERG

"If I have to slide head-first into home, I'll do it. If I have to run through a wall, I'll do it. The money I'm making, I should be willing to take chances."

Pete Rose, baseball's first $100,000 singles hitter, does take chances. He stretches singles into doubles, drops bunts to win batting crowns, and bowls over catchers to win All-Star Games. He's the man who revived the belly-slide and initiated the idea of running out bases on balls.

"Frank Robinson bears down all the time," says Rose of his ex-Cincinnati teammate. "He's like me—all out. A lot of people think I did something dirty in the 1970 All-Star Game when I ran into Ray Fosse. I wasn't being dirty, I was just trying to win."

That incident raised quite a ruckus, but Rose would get attention even without his all-out hustle. He's hit over .300 eight years in a row, collected five 200-hit seasons, played five positions as a major-league regular, and won two batting titles in his 10 years in the majors, all with the Reds.

"Every year when I go to spring training," Rose revealed, "I set certain goals—batting .300, getting over 200 hits, collecting 35 doubles, and close to 10 triples. Those are the things a leadoff hitter should do. I like to bat either first or second because you get that extra turn at the plate.

"I think a .300 average is the secret to a lot of things," he explained further. "It means you're around 200 hits, it means you'll be scoring about 100 runs, and it means that most likely you'll be on a winner. Hitting .300 doesn't mean a thing if you're not playing for a winner."

84

With the switch-hitting Rose at the top of the order, the 1972 Reds not only won the Western Division crown, but also knocked off powerful Pittsburgh in the pennant playoffs and then came within a whisker of winning the World Series, bowing to the Oakland A's in a tight, seven-game set.

Rose was "right on" as far as his seasonal goals for 1972. He batted .307, two points below his lifetime average, and hit 31 doubles, 11 triples, and six home runs. He also knocked in 57 runs, stole 10 bases in 13 attempts, and scored 107 times.

The April ballplayers' strike, which wiped out eight Cincinnati games, cost him his most cherished goal—200 hits. Rose, finishing strong, wound up with 198 hits, still the top figure in baseball.

Pete's career goal is nine 200-hit seasons, a feat achieved only by the great Ty Cobb, whose aggressive style of play has been copied by the Cincinnati outfielder. The 32-year-old Rose needs four more years with 200 hits to tie Cobb.

"I'd like to get 3,000 hits for my career," said the fleet leftfielder, who is well on his way with 1,922 as the 1973 season opened. "And I'd like to average 200 hits a year. I'll need a few big seasons and the next four or five are really important to me."

Pete's go-get-'em style and boundless energy have been his trademarks ever since he broke into pro ball at Geneva of the New York-Penn League in 1960. He is the perfect example of the self-made man. He has overcome adversity on numerous occasions and made maximum use of his skills with bat and glove.

"No one jumped out of their shoes to sign him when he got out of high school," said Cincinnati manager Sparky Anderson. "He made himself into what he is and to do that you've got to be a competitor. No one can judge himself. When you look into that mirror and can say I gave 100 per cent today, you know you've done all you can do. Pete Rose can do that every day."

His fellow players and managers also recognize Pete's drive. They consistently vote him the game's top competitor.

"It's an attitude," suggested Rose, who is called Charley Hustle by his colleagues. "It's wanting to win all the time no matter what the score and being willing to do whatever it takes to produce a win."

To help make Cincinnati a winning club, Rose has moved from second to third to the outfield—all three outfield positions—since arriving in the majors in 1963. He was the N.L.'s Rookie-of-the-Year that season, hitting .273, then slipped four points to .269 the following year, before producing a solid .312 mark in 1965. He's never been under .300 since.

He's not much of a power-hitter, but doesn't have to be. His main job is to get on base in front of Johnny Bench and Tony Perez.

Nonetheless, Rose has belted two key World Series homers—his Game 5 homer against Oakland last fall was the difference in a 5-4 Reds win—and he twice hit 16 during the regular season.

"If Pete wanted to go for home runs," his manager says, "he could hit 25 of them a season. But it would be the worst thing he could do."

The biggest advantage of the Reds' Riverfront Stadium for Rose is the AstroTurf infield. Ground balls tear through like a rocket, adding points to the averages of hitters who specialize in the ground single or low line drive.

"It's a dream playing at Riverfront with that AstroTurf over the whole field," Rose reported, explaining that the smooth surface also makes his job easier in the outfield. "You can really be an aggressive player because you know there won't be any bad hops. You don't have to worry about the ball hitting a rock and bouncing over your head."

Rose, born and raised in Cincinnati, has a sizable personal cheering section at Riverfront. He's the team captain of the Reds and top cheerleader for Sparky Anderson on the field. When he gets on base, he claps his hands and shouts encouragement to his teammates. What he's saying is, "Keep it going! Get me home!"

After Cincinnati won the National League championship in 1970, Rose reflected on the season's personal significance to him.

"I grew up just a few miles from Riverfront Stadium and that really made the season special for me," he said. "It was the kind of year you dream about—what with the opening of the new stadium, hosting the All-Star Game, and winning the Western Division and N.L. playoffs. Of course, we didn't look like the Big Red Machine against Baltimore. But that was just one of those things."

It was in that 1970 All-Star Game that Rose had his famous collision with Ray Fosse in the bottom of the 12th inning. The Cincinnati star slammed into the Cleveland catcher, jarring the ball loose and winning the game for the Nationals, 5-4. The incident, which sidelined Fosse when the regular schedule resumed, angered the American League All-Stars.

One of those most upset was Fosse, who had visited Rose at his home the previous evening. "I don't know," the catcher said later. "Some of the guys on our bench thought he could have gone around me."

Pitcher Clyde Wright, who yielded the single that allowed Rose to reach base, said in disgust, "Why did he have to do that? I guess that's how he plays. But from where I was standing, it looked like he could have gone around him."

To this day, Rose defends himself. "Fosse was a stride up the line and had the baseline completely surrounded," he explains. "I started to slide and I saw I couldn't make it. Head first would've been worse. No way. I just had to run and hit him. I got him with the knee, the whole body, everything."

The late Gil Hodges, who piloted that N.L. All-Star team, also said the Cincinnati outfielder had little choice. "Fosse was in the act of receiving the ball when Pete hit him," said Hodges. "It was just a bit before the ball got to him and it hit his glove or someplace. The boy had the plate blocked, but Pete was going to score one way or another."

Though most fans vividly recall that game when they think of Pete Rose, the Reds' captain rates several other contests as the games he remembers most.

One of the biggest came in 1963, when Rose was a rookie second baseman. His home run at the old Polo Grounds gave Reds ace pitcher Jim Maloney his 20th win that season—1-0.

Another highlight came in 1968, when Rose and Matty Alou, then with Pittsburgh, were battling for the batting crown. Rose, mired in a late-season tailspin, watched his point spread over Alou disappear, until the two men were virtually deadlocked with two games to go in the season.

Finally, in the next-to-last game of the year, Rose broke out of his slump with a flourish, collecting five hits in as many tries against righthander Gaylord Perry, then a Giant. But Alou, hanging tough, went 4-for-4 in his game.

The batting crown was decided on the last day. Rose got one hit in three swings as Alou went 0-for-4, giving the hustling Red standout his first batting championship with a .335 average. Alou hit .332.

In 1969, another Pirate, Roberto Clemente, took Rose down to the wire in the batting race. With the Cincy star guarding a narrow lead on the last day of the season, every at-bat was important.

"I'd gone 0-for-3 when the news came from the press box that Clemente had gone 3-for-3," Rose remembered. "If Clemente had gone 4-for-4 and I had gone 0-for-4, he would've won.

"When I came to bat the fourth time, I was really sweating. I figured that the last thing anybody'd expect in that situation was a bunt, so I laid it down. I never ran so fast to first in my life. I doubt any record-breaking sprinter could have beaten me. When I crossed the bag, I was safe and I had my second straight batting championship."

This time, Rose had hit .348 to Clemente's .345.

Traditionally a slow starter, Rose generally hits in the .280's in April and May, then starts tearing the cover off the ball once the weather warms up. He's been known to hit over .400 in July and August.

"It seems to be in my nature to get off to a slow start," he says. "I prefer to play in warm weather and I seem to have a problem getting loosened up in the spring. I like to play in a T-shirt and I like to perspire when I'm playing."

He struggled to get his 1972 season average to .307, but certainly was loose for the playoffs against the Pirates. He set a championship series record with nine hits—he also hit safely in all five games—including a key RBI double in the finale. In the World Series, however, Oakland pitching kept him down to .214.

"I looked at those ERA's," Rose said of the A's pitching staff, "and I don't care if you're pitching for the Rhode Island Reds in the Chicken League, a good ERA is a good ERA."

Rose was hardly making excuses, and he didn't have to. When he falls victim to a rare slump, the 5-11, 195-pound pepperpot spends hours in the batting cage, trying to find the flaw. A self-taught switch-hitter, he has more power lefthanded, but is equally adept at handling right or lefthanded pitching, as his batting average against each shows.

In addition to winning games—and pennants—with his bat and glove, Pete Rose will use psychological warfare on the opposition if he feels it will help. And, after a quick study of the A's pitching last fall, Rose resorted to such a tactic.

He got Oakland's ace, Catfish Hunter, so mad that Hunter threatened to deck Rose the next time they faced each other. What did Rose say? "Catfish Hunter is good, but he's not a super-pitcher. He's like Rick Wise of the Cardinals in our own league."

Wise was, indeed, a good pitcher, but nothing more. He'd posted a 16-16 mark and 3.11 ERA for St. Louis.

But Hunter, escaping Vida Blue's shadow to emerge as the A's ace, had a sensational year with a 21-7 mark, including five shutouts, and a brilliant 2.04 ERA, third best in the A.L.

Rose also angered the A's by saying prior to the Series, "Well, the two best teams have already played. Us and Pittsburgh."

The icing on the cake was a knock on the whole American League. "People ask me every year if I'll get my 200 hits," he said. "Now how many players get asked that question in the American League?"

His unkind comments about the American League and its champs stirred the ire of the normally placid Oakland fans, who pelted Pete with vegetables and fruit when he assumed his left field position in the Oakland Coliseum.

"This was vegetable day," laughed Rose, after his three hits led the Reds to victory in Game 5 and the A's fans responded in kind. "Thursday, they were throwing oranges and apples, but today it was tomatoes and eggs."

Rose scored a run and knocked in two others in the game. "His leadoff homer did a lot for our dugout," Sparky Anderson said, after Rose had tagged Hunter's first pitch of the game.

In the ninth, with Cesar Geronimo on second and Dave Concepcion on first, Rose banged a single up the middle off ace reliever Rollie Fingers to score the winning run.

Performances like that have earned Pete his estimated

$115,000 salary, tops in the singles-hitters' league. He attributes his success on the diamond to his love for the game.

"I just love to play baseball," says Rose. "It isn't just a job with me. When it's fun, that's the way you play, with the hustling and all."

Rose's hustle combined with his natural talents to give the Reds the best leadoff man in baseball in 1972. Together with Joe Morgan and Bobby Tolan, Cincy's second and third hitters, the three men at the top of the order were on base 782 times during the year, giving sluggers Johnny Bench and Tony Perez ample opportunity to drive them in.

"I figure," says Sparky Anderson, "that if Rose, Morgan, and Tolan can get on base five times a game among them, that we'll win." He's often right.

When the trio was held in check by Oakland in the first four games of the 1972 World Series, the Reds could manage only one win, a 1-0 nerve-racker thrown by journeyman Jack Billingham.

"We're flat," said a disappointed Rose after the A's took a 3-1 lead in the best-of-seven Fall Classic. "That's a good word for it. We don't have any momentum. Everybody's sitting here waiting for things to happen, but in baseball you can't do that. If you just sit there and wait, they don't happen."

Rose doesn't sit around and wait. He runs to the plate, waves the bat, and looks for a way—any way—to get on base. He led the Reds in getting hit by a pitch in 1972, among other things. His 100-plus runs scored marked the fifth time in his career he's done that, a remarkable achievement.

He's been the team's Most Valuable Player on three different occasions (1966, 1968, 1969) and holds numerous club records, including most hits collected in a Cincinnati uniform, 1,922. He gained first place in the Reds' hit parade this past season, topping Vada Pinson and Ed Roush. Rose ranks second to Frank Robinson in runs scored for the Reds and third, behind Pinson and Robinson, in Cincinnati doubles.

At 32, Rose is the second oldest regular on the club (third baseman Denis Menke is one year older), leading the sparkplug captain to say, "I think we have the makings of a dynasty if you examine our personnel."

Baseball people have learned to be skeptical, because the Cardinals, Mets, and Orioles of recent years—and the 1972 Pirates—made similar claims which dissolved surprisingly fast. Still, Rose insists.

"Our manager, Sparky Anderson, he's like me," Rose says. "He hates to lose, but figures like I do that if you get beat on Monday, you go back out there and get them on Tuesday."

The son of a top semipro ballplayer who was well-known in Cincinnati, Rose is at the peak of his popularity today, but he's always one step ahead, always thinking about tomorrow. And what's in his future? For one thing, he says he'd like to manage the Reds.

Rose, the ballplayer, is truly made of managerial timber, but so long as he's still getting good wood on the ball, hustling No. 14 will remain on the playing field, not in the dugout. Besides, Sparky Anderson is hardly ready for retirement with two pennants in three seasons under his belt since relieving Dave Bristol as Cincy pilot.

Meanwhile, Rose will continue to be the eternal optimist and go-getter of the Reds, an inspirational player to teammates, rivals, and fans alike. It's the only way he knows how to play.

"Rose plays the game like it should be played," writes Atlanta Braves traveling secretary Don Davidson in his book, *Caught Short*. "I have never seen him loaf while on the baseball field; he never runs to first when he receives a base on balls.

"I advise youngsters to watch Pete Rose in action and take a cue from him. They'll have a running start toward the major leagues and, perhaps, a six-figure salary."

PETE ROSE

Year	Club	Lea	Pos	AB	R	H	HR	RBI	Avg.
1960	Geneva	N. Y.-Pa.	2B	321	60	89	1	43	.277
1961	Tampa	Fla. St.	2B	484	105	160	2	77	.331
1962	Macon	So. Atl.	2B	540	136	178	9	71	.330
1963	Cincinnati	N. L.	2B-OF	623	101	170	6	41	.273
1964	Cincinnati	N. L.	2B	516	64	139	4	34	.269
1965	Cincinnati	N. L.	2B	670	117	209	11	81	.312
1966	Cincinnati	N. L.	2B-3B	654	97	205	16	70	.313
1967	Cincinnati	N. L.	OF-2B	585	86	176	12	76	.301
1968	Cincinnati	N. L.	OF-2B-1B	626	94	210	10	49	.335
1969	Cincinnati	N. L.	OF-2B	627	120	218	16	82	.348
1970	Cincinnati	N. L.	OF	649	120	205	15	52	.316
1971	Cincinnati	N. L.	OF	632	86	192	13	44	.304
1972	Cincinnati	N. L.	OF	645	107	198	6	57	.307
	World Series								
1970	Cincinnati	N. L.	OF	20	2	5	1	2	.250
1972	Cincinnati	N. L.	OF	28	3	6	1	2	.214

NOLAN RYAN

The Untouchable

by ARNOLD HANO

Nolan Ryan is just a nice-looking kid who happens to throw a baseball faster than any other resident of tiny Alvin, Texas.

Nolan Ryan is simply a flame-thrower. They call him The Express. Get it? Ryan's Express. Harmon Killebrew says if he ever gets hit with Ryan's express, he'll have the pitcher arrested for manslaughter. Oakland slugger Reggie Jackson says Ryan is the only pitcher he's afraid of, down-deep-in-the-guts afraid of. "If a pitch ever gets away from him, he will kill someone."

Nolan Ryan pitches for the California Angels, in Anaheim, which you also wouldn't confuse with New York. Thus, few people really know what an exciting young man this is, perhaps the most exciting single performer in baseball today. Yes, I've heard of Hank Aaron. For years I beat the drums, by myself, for Roberto Clemente. I like the cool gall of Vida Blue, the hot moxie of Pete Rose. They all excite me. But not down deep in the guts, the way this kid does. He excites me. He frightens me. He puts me on that double-pronged fork of attraction and revulsion. When you watch Nolan Ryan rear and throw that screaming blur of white toward the plate, you don't know whether to watch or cover your eyes. Will he strike out the hitter, or will he strike him dead?

You know that Ryan struck out 329 men last season, best in the majors, fourth best in major league history. Do you know he also walked 157 men? Nobody in baseball was close. You walk 100 batters in a season, and you're a wild man. You walk 150 batters, and they let you out of your cage only under armed guard. Scary.

Let's flit through the stats, briefly, so you'll see why we've got this young man in this book. He won 19 games last year. He pitched 20 complete games; only two men, Cy Young winner Gaylord Perry and Detroit's Mickey Lolich, pitched more. He led his league in shutouts, with nine, and tied Don Sutton and Steve Carlton for the major league lead. He compiled his league's seventh best earned run average, a stingy 2.28. And he struck out batters at a rate of 10.44 per every nine innings, bested only by Sam McDowell's 10.71 in 1965. Sandy Koufax never struck out men as fast.

He is not yet the best pitcher in the American League. But he threatens to be, very soon. At the end of last season, a group of big-league pitching coaches got together to determine the best pitcher in baseball. You can guess the names that popped up: Lolich, Seaver, Gibson, Carlton, Jenkins, Wood, Palmer, McNally. That's the order the coaches placed them. Plus one other guy, "perhaps surprisingly," was the way one magazine put it, "California's Nolan Ryan."

Of Ryan, the magazine said, "No pitcher has fewer credentials, but more potential."

The credentials are there, if you will look. How many pitchers have ever struck out 21 men in any game, sandlot, minor-league, college ball, or big-league? Ryan struck out 21, while toiling for Greenville, in the Western Carolinas A league in 1966, a 19-year-old kid. Naturally, he lost the game, 2-1. Two men stole home on Ryan. At Greenville, Ryan hurled 183 innings and struck out 272 men, over 13 men for every nine innings pitched. He's done better. In a brief stint with Jacksonville, in the International League in 1967, Ryan shot down 18 men in seven innings, better than two men an inning.

That was minor-league stuff. This past season he whiffed 17 men in one game, to tie a league record for strikeouts at night. Twice he got 16 men. A game against Boston on July 9 has to be one of the finest any man has thrown. He walked leadoff hitter Tommy Harper. He struck out Doug Griffin. Carl Yastrzemski singled cleanly. Period. Ryan closed the books on Boston, then and there. He struck out Reggie Smith and Rico Petrocelli, to end the first inning. He struck out Carlton Fisk, Bob Burda, and Juan Beniquez, on nine pitches, in the second inning. That's not the first time he's fanned the side. He's done it 20 times. It's not even the first time he's struck out the side on nine pitches. He did that once before. He struck out eight men in a row that day, for an American League record. He retired the last 26 men in order.

In the old days, when Ryan was a thrower for the New York Mets, he had a rep for fading away at the season's end. This past year, working 130-plus innings more than he'd ever pitched in a single season, he shot for his 20th win on the last game of the campaign. But Oakland beat him, 2-1. One run was unearned, in typical Ryan fashion. He tried to pick a man off first, and threw the ball away. The man moved into scoring position, where he later scored. Ryan gave up five hits that day, three walks, 10 strikeouts. A typical Ryan performance in every way. The time before, on September 30, he beat Minnesota, 3-2, and fanned 17.

That's fading away like Christy Mathewson.

So the credentials are there. He set 11 club records. In one string he ripped off 15 straight hitless innings. He threw three straight shutouts. Six times his team was shut out with Ryan pitching; in those six games, Ryan's ERA was a measly 1.17. He could have—should have—won all six. Twice he had no-hitters into the eighth inning. He lost one of those games, without the benefit of a hit. Against Kansas City on July 31, he walked Amos Otis in the fourth inning. Ryan tried to pick Otis off first and threw the ball away, a trick Ryan performs with alarming regularity. Otis wound up at third. With two out, and Otis still on third, Ryan went 3-and-2 on John Mayberry, a big lefthanded hitter. Nobody ever steals on the 3-2 count, with two out, and few people steal with a lefthanded hitter up; the catcher has too clear a view of the runner coming down. Otis stole home, on ball four to Mayberry. Kansas City won, 1-0, its only hit a meaningless single by Steve Hovley in the eighth. Ryan committed three errors that night.

Yes, the credentials are there. And no doubt about the potential. And no doubt about Ryan's imperfections and unceasing poor luck.

How did it happen? How has this youngster escaped attention? Easy. He got buried in New York. Stars become superstars in New York, but also-rans end up last.

This past season at Anaheim, pitching coach Tom Morgan did wonderful things with young Ryan, smoothing the delivery, improving the timing. Ryan is grateful. "But I don't rate it on a par with pitching every four days. That's what *really* did it for me."

What didn't do it for Ryan—he says—was pitching "every 10th or 12th day" when he was a Met. It's the same old story. A young, wild-flinging fireballer can't throw the ball over the plate, so his manager won't risk using him too often. But unless the wild flinger works regularly, he can't learn to throw the ball over the plate. A vicious cycle. It took Sandy Koufax five years to break out of that rut. Nolan Ryan spent four seasons with the Mets, locked in that same cycle. He never pitched more than 152 innings in any season. He lost more games than he won. The most games he won as a Met was 10. In 1971 he walked seven men every nine innings. That's wild. Oh, he had his moments. He won a game for the Mets in the 1969 playoffs against the Braves, going seven innings in relief, striking out seven, giving up just three hits. He pitched 2⅓ innings in the World Series, and held Baltimore scoreless. Nobody doubted he could get you out, if he got the ball over. It was always too big an if for the Mets.

On December 10, 1971, the Mets unloaded Ryan, together with minor-league pitcher Don Rose, catcher Francisco Estrada and outfielder Leroy Stanton, to the California Angels, for seasoned Jim Fregosi. The Mets gloated. They had sent, it seemed, a bundle of question marks to the Angels for an established star. True, some people thought Fregosi had seen his best days, but he was just 29 years old. How washed up can you be at 29?

Very, it appears.

And the Angels ended up benefiting from one of the most one-sided deals in recent years.

Still, Ryan had his problems. He pulled a groin muscle and missed 10 days. Later, his elbow turned tender, and he labored, going a month without a victory. But he managed. Take the elbow. Ryan uses snake oil on the joint. Seems he went hunting with an old codger back in Texas one winter, and the old codger had bad arthritis. They came across a rattlesnake, and the o.c. killed the snake, but salvaged the oil, and boiled it. Then he rubbed the oil into his arthritis, and, by gum, soon he was dancing a jig. Ryan was impressed. Now he rubs his own snake oil into his joints and adds a heating pad.

So fellow Angel pitcher Clyde Wright calls Nolan Ryan, "Dr. Snake Oil." Other people call him other names. Rudy May calls him, "Greatness." And Harry Dalton, general manager of the Angels, calls him "Untouchable."

Which is what he is these days. Pitching coach Tom Morgan says if he had to pick a pitcher to throw just one pitch upon which a game turned, he'd call on Ryan. (With an if, naturally.) "*If* Ryan got that one pitch over with the stuff he has, no one would touch him." That's one kind of untouchable. GM Dalton means that the youngster will not be traded or sold under any circumstances. Untouchable.

Meanwhile, Tom Morgan is trying to teach the young man to control his stuff better. After the control, comes a changeup. And if you ever see Nolan Ryan throwing his heat where he wants to, and mixing in an occasional change, forget Lolich and Seaver and Jenkins and all the rest. The Express will be on the track. Heck, even without control and change, he's highballing right along. He may be to his league what Bob Feller was 30 years ago. He may be to baseball what Sandy Koufax was 10 years ago.

Pure excitement.

ARNOLD HANO is the author of a number of widely praised books on baseball and hundreds of magazine articles. His home nest is in Laguna Beach, California.

NOLAN RYAN

Year	Club	Lea	IP	W	L	SO	BB	H	ERA
1965	Marion _____	Appal.	78	3	6	115	56	61	4.38
1966	Greenville _____	W. Carolinas	183	17	2	272	127	109	2.51
1966	Williamsport _____	Eastern	19	0	2	35	12	9	0.95
1966	New York _____	N. L.	3	0	1	6	3	5	15.00
1967	Winter Haven _____	Fla.-St.	4	0	0	5	2	1	2.25
1967	Jacksonville _____	Int.	7	1	0	18	3	3	0.00
1968	New York _____	N. L.	134	6	9	133	75	93	3.09
1969	New York _____	N. L.	89	6	3	92	53	60	3.54
1970	New York _____	N. L.	132	7	11	125	97	86	3.41
1971	New York _____	N. L.	152	10	14	137	116	125	3.97
1972	California _____	A. L.	284	19	16	329	156	166	2.28
	World Series								
1969	New York _____	N. L.	2⅓	0	0	3	2	1	0.00

GENE TENACE

Assassin's Target

by RAY ROBINSON

So the guys with the long scraggly hair, the mutton
chops a la Martin Van Buren and the Mexican bandit
spit-curl mustaches won it all! It took seven games, six
won by one hairy run—as everyone knows—and Fury
Gene Tenace suddenly became a household word. The
jokes about his name—"Tennis, anyone?" and Tenace the
Menace—competed with tales about how he was suddenly
a threat to the memory of Babe Ruth. And it was
generally conceded that nobody in a World Series had
ever spent a more profitable seven days in becoming
glamorous, not even the hook-nosed Gashouser Pepper
Martin back in 1931 for the St. Louis Cardinals, or, for
that matter, Roberto Clemente in 1971.

Vida Blue, Joe Rudi, Rollie Fingers, Sal Bando, Mike
Epstein, Catfish Hunter—they might all have been more
logical candidates for stardom in the 1972 series. But in
the final analysis, it turned out to be Gene Tenace, as
unknown before the World Series as Spiro Agnew was
before Richard Nixon anointed him for the Vice Presiden-
tial nomination in 1968. Not even the late Gen. William
Eckert—"The Unknown Soldier"—suffered from equal
obscurity when baseball's establishment chose him to serve
as Baseball Commissioner before the current reign of
Bowie Kuhn.

But by the end of the sixth game of the 1972 Series
Gene Tenace and his droopy mustache had not only
become famous and productive, he had also become the
target of a potential assassin. When one becomes a
household world in America these days, then it seems
armed reptiles get set to strike back. Thus, in accordance

97

with such contemporary sociological rules, the hirsute catcher of the Athletics, had his life threatened.

The would-be culprit was a 32-year-old Louisville gun-toter who, while waiting on a Cincinnati standing-room line for the sixth game, proclaimed menacingly to a nearby woman, that "if Tenace hits a home run today, he won't walk out of this ball park." The woman tipped off police officials about the threat and a quick search of the man's pockets revealed that he was carrying a loaded pistol and a whiskey bottle.

After the game, when Tenace was filled in about the threat, he said: "It's a terrible situation. The guy's got to be mentally disturbed to think about something like that. But I'm not going to let it interfere with my playing tomorrow."

Tomorrow, of course, turned out to be the decisive seventh game of the World Series. And icy-veined Gene was absolutely true to his word. Not only did he comport himself with reasonable alacrity at first base, where man-ager Dick Williams of Oakland installed him in a shook-up lineup, but he was also placed at the cleanup spot in the batting order, instead of the seventh rung he had occupied in the first six games. Batting fourth, Tenace went two-for-three, including a sixth inning double down the left-field line that gave the Athletics a 2-1 lead that they never relinquished. The final score was 3-2, Oakland had won the world title and Gene Tenace was the undisputed hero of the classic. With it, of course, went the traditional garnishing of the MVP car, the plaudits of the sports world and some excessive bear hugs from Charles Oscar Finley, the brash and controversial self-made millionaire owner of the A's.

Tenace, positively amazed at his own post-season mag-nificence, which included four home runs, tying the series record shared by four others, including Babe Ruth and Lou Gehrig, had banged in nine runs out of the meager total of 16 that Oakland's batting cast had produced throughout the Series. Nobody else on Oakland had more than one run batted in.

Cincinnati's second baseman, Joe Morgan, summed up his team's—and perhaps the entire civilized world's—atti-tude towards the quirky emergence of this 26-year-old athlete. "We let one guy beat us," he said, disappointedly. "It's all right if all their guys hit and beat us but Tenace is the only one who did it. I just don't believe in letting one guy beat you."

Sportswriter Jim Murray of the Los Angeles Times analogized what crimes Tenace had committed against the disgusted Reds to "losing a poker game to a guy who keeps saying 'Are these cards any good? I haven't played this game very much.' "

As far as his own attitude was concerned, Tenace celebrated his new-found profile as home run slugger and .348 hitter, with becoming modesty. "It takes 25 players to win a Series," he said. "Fortunately, I had a tremendous Series. But as far as being a hero, I don't really look at it that way. It's not going to change anything. I'm still going to be me."

That assessment may not be quite accurate, of course. For Charlie Finley is bound to pay more money in 1973 to Gene Tenace, who earned about $18,000 regular pay in '72, before Finley's magnanimity during the Series produced an extra $5000 for him. Also, there is every reason to suspect that Tenace's obvious flaws as a catcher—his inability to cut down runners on the bases and his butterfingers on low wild pitches—might force manager Williams to consider a switch of his Series hero to first base. With Mike Epstein being traded off to the Texas Rangers and Mike Hegan generally being rated as a good-field, no-hit first baseman, Gene might be a natural for that post—if, of course, Dave Duncan, who began 1972 as Oakland's first-string catcher, can bat his way back to his regular job behind the plate.

Now that Gene Tenace has graduated into baseball's mythology, it is necessary to take a closer look at the legend and the record. After all, there was a certain amount of exaggeration connected with his sudden rise to eminence. The exaggeration has to do mainly with those judgments on the part of fellow pros and press that Gene Tenace, prior to the Series, was little more than just another ballplayer and, therefore, an unlikely hero, to say the least. Typical of such disparagements was one remark about Tenace that complimented him for having his average climb "clear up over .200" on several previous occasions. A more honest scrutiny of Tenace's major and minor league record indicates that such an appraisal is akin to campaign rhetoric.

For instance, in his first two years in Oakland, Gene

batted .305 in 1970, with seven homers in 105 times at bat and .274 in 1971, with seven homers in 179 times at bat. This doesn't exactly make Tenace a threat to Babe Ruth or even, for that matter, to Mike Epstein. But it also doesn't make him a .200 hitter. One year in the minors— 1969 with Birmingham in the Southern Association—Tenace batted .319, with 20 home runs in only 276 times at bat. That happens to be a ration of one homer to every 14 at bats. In most circles, that is considered the true index of a bona fide slugger. His top home run achievement was in 1968, when he connected 21 times for Peninsula in the Carolina League.

So a close examination of the eight-year baseball career of Tenace indicates that he is, in reality, not quite the cipher and mediocrity he has been cracked up to be by a press always eager to create a Cinderella story overnight.

If anything, there is reason to believe that Tenace, with his new-found confidence, might seriously contend with Reggie Jackson, who was sidelined during the World Series, for the role as Oakland's best slugger in the years to come. On the other hand, Tenace might be every bit as bad as he's rumored to be in the defensive department. The Reds proved this by running against him with impunity in the Series. Then, when Dick Williams put Gene at first base in the seventh game of the Series ("They'll have me playing goalie next," muttered Gene before the game), he left him in there only long enough to break up the contest with his bat. By the sixth inning, when Gene was perched at second base, after his game-winning double, Williams pulled him out of there for a pinch-runner, Allen Lewis. But Williams probably was more concerned at that time with defensing first base in the last crucial innings of the game, as Mike Hegan took over at that slot in the bottom of the inning.

Tenace didn't like it, either. "I was upset that I was taken out," said Gene. "I wanted to stay in the lineup and play. I wanted to be out there when we won it or lost it. I felt I could score as well as anyone else on the team. When I saw Lewis coming out, I couldn't believe it. I was really disappointed."

On the other hand, Williams thought it was a perfectly logical move to make. "Tenace was coming out of the game, anyway," he said. "We had a one-run lead and I've got to go with my defense—Hegan at first."

The man with the hot hand in the '72 Series came into that competition with a .225 average and only five home runs during the regular season. Against the Detroit Tigers in a spirited American League playoff, Gene was futile, going just one for 16, for an average of .062. However, his lone hit of the playoffs arrived just in the nick of time: it won Game Five, 2-1, at Detroit. It also saved Gene, as well as his manager, from a volley of criticism, for in Game Four, Williams installed Tenace at second base in the late innings. That was just long enough for Gene to drop a throw as the pivot man in a double play during the Tigers' three-run tenth inning rally that produced a win to keep the Tigers alive in the playoffs.

That lapse was immediately forgotten, once the World Series got under way, when, in his first two times at bat against Cincinnati, before the Reds' home fans, Tenace unloaded two home runs against Gary Nolan. The blows won the ball game against the heavily-favored Reds, 3-2, and also seemed to presage impending doom for a ball club, that man-for-man, was considered far superior to Oakland's collection. In addition, the home runs provided Gene with that most curious of all records: he was the first man ever to hit home runs in his first two appearances at the plate in a Series game. Gene added homers in the fourth game and the fifth game, to give him his amazing bag of four for the set.

Gene Tenace, whose family name was originally Fiore Gino Tenace, (pronounced Ten-a-chee), grew up in Lucasville, Ohio, some 100 miles from Cincinnati. His paternal grandfather, who came from Italy, settled in Pittsburgh and died in a coal-mine accident. The young man also spent time in his youth in Russelton, Pennsylvania, a locale in which the New York Yankees operated a farm club in Butler, Pa. As a kid, Gene was a Yankee fan, possibly because of the proximity of the Butler club and also because the Yankees had mined for stardom some of the greatest Italo-American players in the game's history, including Tony Lazzeri, Joe DiMaggio, Frankie Crosetti, Phil Rizzuto, Yogi Berra and Vic Raschi. However, when Yankee scouts looked Gene over, they found him as wanting as did most of the sport's journalists prior to the World Series of last fall. Expressing no interest in the boy, the Yanks were content to let Tenace be signed by Danny Carnevale, a scout for the Kansas City Athletics, which utimately became Oakland's big league franchise.

Gene's Dad was also a ballplayer—and, according to Gene, a "pretty good one." "When I was a kid," recalls Gene, "my Dad was a semi-pro and he drove me to become a big leaguer. When I say drove, I'm not kidding, either. When I was in the Little League, he was on me all the time, always telling me to do better. Maybe that's why I had an ulcer when I was a teen-ager. I don't have one now. But I did then."

Curiously enough, Cincinnati scouts, as well as Yankee scouts had looked at Tenace and didn't like what they saw. Gene Bennett, a Reds' bird dog, caught Gene's act and said the boy couldn't cut it.

Fame, now that it has come for Fury Gene Tenace, may be very fleeting. Other World Series heroes like Al Gionfriddo, Sandy Amoros, Cookie Lavagetto and Gene Bearden left few foot prints of greatness after their spectacular Series performances. But Tenace could be different. He's young and willing and loves to hit. Zeal and desire won't hurt him in the long run.

He also can reap additional satisfaction out of knowing that he didn't find it necessary to play ball in the Caribbean this past winter. He just didn't have to make the extra money this time around.

And there might have been some perverse pleasure in knowing, as his teammate Reggie Jackson reminded him, that if he was going to be gunned down by some assassin during the 1972 Series, "at least it would have been on national television."

"No one would have bothered shooting me," added Mike Epstein, the man who couldn't buy a hit in the same Series in which Gene Tenace simply couldn't resist staying out of the action.

GENE TENACE

Year	Club	Lea	Pos	AB	R	H	HR	RBI	Avg.
1965	Shelby _____	W. Carolinas	OF	93	10	17	2	6	.183
1966	Leesburg _____	Fla. St.	1B-OF-3B-P	228	28	48	1	24	.211
1967	Peninsula _____	Carolina	OF	7	0	0	0	1	.000
1967	Leesburg _____	Fla. St.	OF-C-2-3-P	354	47	94	6	44	.266
1968	Peninsula _____	Carolina	C-OF-3-1-P	435	78	123	21	71	.283
1969	Birmingham _____	Southern	C-OF-3B	276	56	88	20	74	.319
1969	Oakland _____	A. L.	C	38	1	6	1	2	.158
1970	Iowa _____	A. A.	C-OF	319	54	90	16	63	.282
1970	Oakland _____	A. L.	C	105	19	32	7	20	.305
1971	Oakland _____	A. L.	C-OF	179	26	49	7	25	.274
1972	Oakland _____	A. L.	C-OF	227	22	51	5	32	.225
	World Series								
1972	Oakland _____	A. L.	C-1B	23	5	8	4	9	.348

LUIS TIANT

Fu Manchu's Comeback

by AL HIRSHBERG

The hottest team in baseball during the last half of the 1972 season was the Boston Red Sox, and the American League's hottest pitcher over the same stretch was Luis Tiant. There was, of course, a close correlation between the success of the ball club and the Cuban's amazing effectiveness. Neither could have functioned as well without the other.

In August and September Tiant won 11 out of 12 games and the Red Sox shot up from a lethargic fourth in the American League East race to the division's top. They led during most of the month of September and lost the title to Detroit only on the next to last day of the season.

There were other factors in their unexpected run for the roses, but the most important cog in the club's pitching wheel was the veteran right-hander who only a year before couldn't even make it to the Atlanta Braves' Triple A farm club in Richmond. The Tiant story was one of the strangest and most gratifying of the year.

Once an outstanding pitcher for the Cleveland Indians, where he won 21 games and led the league in shutouts in 1968, Tiant suddenly developed a sore arm which plagued him for the next three years. As he bounced around from Cleveland to Minnesota to Richmond he failed to make a dent anywhere. The Red Sox picked him up after Richmond released him in 1971. He pitched a short time for Boston's Louisville farm, and finally arrived at Fenway Park in mid-season.

Tiant didn't look any better in Boston than anywhere else. With a 1-7 won-and-lost record and an earned run

103

average of 4.88 for 1971, there was no reason to believe he would help the Red Sox at all in the season to follow. As a matter of fact, Red Sox observers were surprised to see him in spring training.

At Winter Haven, Fla., where the Red Sox train, Tiant was anything but a sure bet to stay with the ball club. Although the club needed pitching, nobody in charge had much hope of Tiant providing any real help. Sonny Siebert and Ray Culp were then the club's twin aces, and several rookies showed promise. Tiant was just on hand, a journeyman who, at 31, was fighting to keep afloat in major league waters.

He made the club, but not by much. When the team went north for the opening of the strike-delayed 1972 season, Tiant was labeled a long middle reliever and possibly a spot starter. But this was more or less an arbitrary designation. Those who knew—or thought they knew—anything about the ball club didn't expect Tiant to be around by Memorial Day.

Three things happened that transformed Tiant from an aging also-ran to the toast of the town. The first was Sonny Siebert's mystifying mound collapse. Siebert, a stalwart on the Red Sox pitching staff for nearly three years, had a rough time getting started. He ended up with a fairly respectable 12-12 mark, but in the early days of the season he was in and out.

Far more disastrous to the Red Sox than Siebert's problem was Ray Culp's sore arm. The right-hander had had a losing season in 1971, but, like Siebert, was considered a top member of the staff. He had overcome previous arm trouble and, in fact, had had few complaints during his Red Sox years. Now, however, he was nearly useless. Long before the season ended, he underwent surgery and was lost for the year. Later, convinced he would never come back, the Red Sox released him.

The loss of Culp and the troubles of Siebert left wide gaps in Boston's pitching rotation. With only Marty Pattin, obtained in an off-season trade, to depend on, manager Eddie Kasko was desperate for help. He turned to Tiant because of a few good showings in relief and the Cuban's own assurance that his arm seemed to be coming back.

Kasko finally put Tiant into the starting rotation soon after the All-Star game. Besides Pattin and Siebert, the other starters were rookies, John Curtis and Lynn

McGlothen. Within a couple of weeks, Tiant appeared to be better than any of them and before the season was over he had proved it.

A minor figure in the Red Sox picture for so long that only his teammates seemed to know he was there, Tiant suddenly became not only the biggest winner on the pitching staff, but the most colorful personality in the locker room.

He grew a Fu Manchu mustache. He smoked cigars in the shower. He clowned around, needling teammates unmercifully in his heavily-accented English. On August 1, he went too far with Reggie Smith, the switch-hitting outfielder, and the two started a fist fight in the runway between the locker room and the dugout. It was quickly broken up, and later Tiant won the ball game with Smith driving home the winning run.

The unpleasantness with Smith turned out to be nothing more than a flareup. Once over, it was forgotten. Tiant continued to clown, ride everyone in sight, smoke cigars in showers—and win ball games. That was most important of all. A completely healthy Tiant was a fine pitcher, and by mid-summer the Cuban was completely healthy.

After his August 1 victory, he went into an almost unbelievable streak, during which six of his next eight starts were shutout victories. In Chicago one night, he went to the eighth inning before giving a hit to the White Sox. Soon after that, he held the Orioles hitless through nearly seven innings in Baltimore. The Chicago game ended up a two-hitter for Tiant and the Baltimore game a three-hitter.

Almost single-handed, he pitched the Red Sox into first place in the American League East. His streak continued through September and his triumphs were mostly where they counted—against A.L. East clubs. He was especially effective against contending teams in that division—the Orioles, the Tigers and the Yankees. They, along with the Red Sox, conducted a four-team dog fight for the championship.

By the end of the 1972 season, Tiant was the American Leagues' leading pitcher with a 1.91 earned run average. With 15 wins, six losses and three saves, he was also high in that department, too. If he had pitched as often in the first half of the season as he did in the last, there is no way of knowing how far he would have gone.

"I could have been in the starting rotation right from the beginning," he said. "I pitched well in Winter Haven, and my arm never bothered me."

While he was having arm trouble, nobody objected to his gyrations on the mound, some of which may be on the edge of legality. He wiggles just about everything, especially with men on bases. When he comes down from the stretch, his glove shimmies so much he seems to have lost control of it.

All of which drives hitters crazy because he wrecks their concentration. There is something morbidly fascinating about Tiant's moves. He hypnotizes the opposition with them, and when he suddenly lets his pitches go, all but the best hitters are usually caught off stride.

The protests that emanate both from the batter's box and the bench worry Tiant not at all. He had to put up with them during his great 1968 season, and he knows that as long as he wins he'll have to put up with them again. It doesn't bother him, and apparently it doesn't bother the umpires either. They are satisfied that his unusual motion is perfectly legal.

He has a wide repertoire of pitches, including a hesitation reminiscent of Satchel Paige. In his few major league years, Paige was constantly under attack by opposing managers and batters. The skinny right-hander, who saw his best days in the old Negro leagues before organized baseball removed the color line, also depended heavily on unorthodox moves on the mound.

Like Paige, Tiant, at his best, has pin-point control. He wastes few pitches, as proved by his 1972 figures. In the 179 innings he pitched, he gave but 65 walks and struck out 123 men. Considering the difference in the amount of work he did, this compared favorably with his 1968 season at Cleveland. In 258 innings that year he fanned 264 men and gave up 73 walks. As in 1972, he led the American League in ERA with a 1.60 mark. The only reason he failed to win the Cy Young Award was that was the year Denny McLain won 31 games for the pennant-winning Tigers.

Because his great effectiveness was confined almost exclusively to the second half of the 1972 season, Tiant had no chance for the Cy Young Award. However, he ended up sixth (Gaylord Perry of Cleveland won it), which in itself was remarkable. That meant his leap from obscurity and a sore-arm history at the start of the year carried him to the top half-dozen pitchers in the American League at the finish.

Tiant's incredible comeback was marred only slightly by his failure to beat the Tigers in the next to last game of the season. Kasko saved him for this clutch contest, but the Red Sox themselves simply didn't have Detroit's depth. Considering the fact that the Tigers were among the favorites to win the division title and the Red Sox weren't supposed to go anywhere, the very fact that the race came down to this game was typical of the surprises provided American League opponents by the Boston club.

As a matter of fact, Tiant, who went 6⅓ innings in that game, might have pulled it out if his mates had hit behind him and if the usually reliable Luis Aparicio hadn't slipped rounding third base on his way to the tying run. The Red Sox finally lost it, 3-1, but the game could as well have gone their way. The last game of the season, meaningless since the Tigers had already clinched the division championship, was easily won by the Red Sox, leaving them only a half-game behind the winners at the finish.

Tiant had more than one reason for being disappointed at his failure to pitch the Red Sox to a pennant. He had hoped that helping to get the club into the World Series might mean a chance for his father to come to the States from Cuba to see him in action.

"My father was a professional ballplayer," he said. "He taught me to pitch and I still use some of the techniques he gave me. We haven't seen each other for many years, but I still have hopes we'll get together. Nothing would please him more than to see me pitch in a World Series." But Tiant has never been on a pennant-winning team.

The fun-loving Luis, who never lost his sense of humor even when things were going badly for him in Boston, spent the winter pitching in the Venezuela League. There, he often saw Red Sox teammate Luis Aparicio, who runs the club in his native Maracaibo. They probably spent most of the winter re-hashing the game in Detroit which cost them a shot at the American League pennant.

Perhaps they'll get that series shot in 1972. The Red Sox team which came north from Winter Haven this year was a far better one than the club Kasko took north with him in 1972. And one of the principal reasons for its improvement was Tiant.

Assuming that his arm remains sound, he will probably be the ace of the Red Sox pitching staff right from the opening of the season this time. And assuming that he can maintain the pace he held in the last few months of the 1972 campaign, he might yet be able to bring his father out of Cuba for a World Series.

Stranger things have happened—like Tiant's comeback.

AL HIRSHBERG is a veteran Boston free-lance writer who has written an entire shelf of sports books, including his famous best-seller, "Fear Strikes Out."

LUIS TIANT

Year	Club	Lea	IP	W	L	SO	BB	H	ERA
1959	Mexico Tigers	Mexican	184	5	19	98	107	214	5.92
1960	Mexico Tigers	Mexican	180	17	7	107	124	194	4.65
1961	Mexico Tigers	Mexican	145	12	9	141	106	138	3.78
1962	Jacksonville	Int.	1	0	0	0	1	0	0.00
1962	Charleston	Eastern	139	7	8	99	72	141	3.63
1963	Burlington	Carolina	204	14	9	207	81	151	2.56
1964	Portland	P. C.	137	15	1	154	40	88	2.04
1964	Cleveland	A. L.	127	10	4	105	47	94	2.83
1965	Cleveland	A. L.	196	11	11	152	66	166	3.54
1966	Cleveland	A. L.	155	12	11	145	50	121	2.79
1967	Cleveland	A. L.	214	12	9	219	67	177	2.73
1968	Cleveland	A. L.	258	21	9	264	73	152	1.60
1969	Cleveland	A. L.	250	9	20	156	129	229	3.71
1970	Minnesota	A. L.	93	7	3	50	41	84	3.39
1971	Rich.-Louisville	Int.	54	3	5	48	28	47	4.17
1971	Boston	A. L.	72	1	7	59	32	73	4.88
1972	Boston	A. L.	179	15	6	123	65	128	1.91

BILLY WILLIAMS

Swinger in The Windy City

by WILLIAM BARRY FURLONG

The years march quickly now and the machine works so smoothly, so undramatically that you almost forget how it came to greatness. Its name is Billy Williams and it plays left field for the Chicago Cubs—a lean, hard-muscled man with smooth skin and high bones and very little inclination to change. He's 34 now and he's been around so long—performing with such a stunning success—that it is hard to know that others are just discovering what has long been the central fact about Billy Williams: that he is the most efficient, consistent—and largely overlooked—hitting machine in the National League.

It is not that he came to greatness last year. It is that others came to know his greatness. For the statistics were inescapable: Billy Williams had the highest average in the major leagues—.333. He led both leagues in total bases and he was second only to Johnny Bench of Cincinnati in runs batted in: 125-122.

By season's end, the awards were beginning to role in: "Player of the Year" for 1972 by the Sporting News, the National League Batting Trophy, the Associated Press All-Star team, the Fred Hutchinson Memorial Award ("typifies the character and competitive spirit" of the late Cincinnati Red manager). But the most coveted award of all: Most Valuable Player in the National League. That one escaped him. One among the 24 voting baseball writers didn't even list Billy in his top ten.

Nevertheless, it was a fulfilling year in the career of Billy Williams.

For years, there had been a baffling gap between The

Professionals' view of Billy Williams and that of the fans. The Professionals looked upon him as one of those very rare players with the near-perfect swing who could hit anything very far, very often, very consistently:

—"He'll be one of the great ones," said Buzzy Bavasi, then of the Dodgers, now front-office chief of the San Diego Padres, when he first saw Williams in spring training in the youth of his glory.

—"He's like Oscar Robertson in basketball," said Willie Stargell of the Pittsburgh Pirates in asserting Billy was the only possible choice for Most Valuable Player. "He's consistent. He gets his 200 hits a year, his 40 homers, his 100 runs batted in."

Yet the perfection was so effortless—so uncomplicated by a florid or damaging temperament—that many fans barely knew he existed. "Most often," he said one calm summer day last year, "it isn't necessarily the good ballplayer that gets in all the stories. It may be the guy who's just another ballplayer, a mediocre player, but who's always stirring things up or getting into hot water—he's the one who gets all the publicity." That isn't Billy Williams' way: "Billy Williams never gets excited. Never gets mad. Never throws a bat," said Leo Durocher, who managed the Cubs until last mid-season. "You write his name down in the same spot in the lineup card every day and you forget it. He will bat third. He will play left field. And that's all—Billy Williams is a baseball machine."

What kind of machine? Some described it in terms of winding up the Billy Williams doll: "This doll does not have to be wound up. It is self-winding."

The result of all this? The baseball pros admired him deeply—and the fans ignored him. As late as last mid-summer, he ranked no better than No. 4 in the balloting for the outfielders on the National League All-star team—though he was batting and fielding far better than any other outfielder in the league. Manager Sparky Anderson named him to the team—as a manager's choice—but still the fans' fervor was muted. "It appears," said one observer, "that he will have to be satisfied with knowing that year in and year out he is just about the best hitter in baseball."

In a sense, it was a momentary failure that brought him the long-delayed attention this last season. Williams himself defined the technique, almost without thinking: "I think the way you get recognized is if you're a .250 hitter and all of a sudden you're hitting .340," he said. "Everybody wonders, 'Hey, where did this guy come from?' And the writers rush up to find out what changes he'd made and how he accounts for his hot streak, and what he's like."

Last spring, Billy Williams was a .250 hitter—who remade himself.

He opened in a cold streak and it was one of those springs when he stayed cold. (*"Last* spring?" he says with a half-laugh that is soft and warm and non-intrusive. *"Every* spring!") By May 19, he was hitting only .254 and the league leaders of the time were 150-190 points ahead of him. But then he began picking up—an extra hit here, an extra homer there. The difference between a .333 hitter and a .250 hitter—at least among regulars who bat 600 times a year—is just two extra hits every week all through the season. *One* extra hit every three games. By mid-June, Billy had climbed over .300. A month later he was up to .342. There he stayed until the final weeks of the season, when he slipped ever so slightly.

There were, to be sure, some streaks in there—some hot streaks. In a one-week period in July, he hit .500. In a two-week period in July, he hit .458, including five homers, six doubles, and 13 runs batted in. But in there was a streak that made for the greatest day he'd ever had in baseball: he got 8-for-8 against the Houston Astros—two homers, a double, five singles, and four runs batted in. It was still one hit short of a record—eight players have gotten nine hits in a double-header—but it raised his batting average 18 points (to .328) in a single day. "It was a week's work in one day," said Leo Durocher.

But it was not all luck and style. For Billy Williams is a shrewd hitter. He doesn't wait until he gets into the batter's box to begin "solving" the pitcher. He's beginning to "hit mentally" while he's in the dugout and then walking to the on-deck circle and settling down on one knee on the towel in the on-deck circle. In all this time, he's doing two things: (1) he's eliminating all the distractions—"the foot, the face, the little twists and expressions, all the things that a pitcher uses to throw you off"—that can blur his concentration on the ball; and (2) he's studying how the ball moves, what the patterns are that the pitcher is using, how often the pitcher uses his "strong" pitch, and in what situations. As it happens, Williams has not only a "perfect" swing but also a gifted set of reflexes. He can match what he sees to what he needs to do. Some years ago, he was batting in the tenth inning against Bobby Tiefenauer, a knuckleball pitcher in Milwaukee on a 3-and-2 pitch, and he had been setting himself mentally for the knuckler when he *saw* that the ball was not taking the breaks of a knuckler. He perceived that the pitch was going to come up as a slider instead of a knuckler; he adjusted his reflexes—and hit the ball out of the park to win the game, 4-3.

On his 8-for-8 day in 1972, the mental work began a week before the game. "When we were in Cincinnati, I noticed Grady Hatton, the Houston superscout, was there," says Williams. This was the weekend before the Houston series against Chicago and he figured Hatton was there to scout the Cub hitters—finding out what was getting them out. It was important to Houston: at the time, the Astros were still in the race for the Western Division lead in the National League. "Cincinnati was getting me out on slow stuff and I figured Hatton would tip the Astros off to that," says Billy. "So on that first day against the Astros, I lay back so I could hit the slow stuff." He got a homer and a couple of singles. "After that, they went back to the fast stuff. But by that time, I guess I was in the groove."

The man-within-the-machine has always used mind and muscle to achieve his high stature in baseball. For he was not a natural outfielder; he was an infielder as a boy growing up in Whistler, Alabama, just a few miles down the road from Mobile. In fact, he was not even a "career" baseball player: his high school didn't have a baseball team so he played football and he won a first-string assignment as a defensive end the first time he ever tried it—*a 155-pound defensive end*. He was good enough at it to earn a scholarship to Grambling, that crucible of great pro football players. He didn't accept the bid—but it might have been safer. As a child, he'd had a tooth knocked out and his cheek gashed when he was hit by a "stick" in a stickball game. Later he was sliding into second in a kids' game on his front lawn—only second base was a water meter. He did some damage to the water meter and considerably more to his knee. He bears scars to this day from both accidents. The inclination to injury followed into the minor leagues—he sliced open a wrist diving for a ball in his first minor-league game and he jammed his shoulder in Louisville later on, diving after another ball. That left him on the sidelines for six weeks. But in the big leagues, he's been as sturdy as he is consistent: in fact he set the National League record for consecutive games played—1,117—between September, 1963 and September, 1970—and though he suffered often from aches and pains, he remained free of crippling injuries.

The route to that record was not pre-planned. Billy spent his summers after high school playing with the Mobile Barons in the semi-pro circuit in Alabama. One summer, Ivy Griffin, a scout for the Chicago Cubs, came to Mobile to scout Tommy Aaron, the brother of Henry Aaron, who was also playing for the Barons. In watching the ball club, he was caught up with the almost flawless artistry of Williams' swing. It is sharp, economical, beautiful in its brevity: it relies on the wrist-snapping power in his hands and forearms, rather than the uncontrolled muscle of his biceps. The ball is not just hit; it is rammed on a line with such screaming speed that it seems to echo down the corridors of time. They tell the time that Billy hit the wall so hard with one line drive that the ball bounced back to the infield before Billy could round first.

The Cub scout looked for a year and then signed Billy up—for a "bonus" that amounted to a one-way ticket to Ponca City and a 15-cent cigar for Billy's dad. Ponca City was the first in a series of minor league stops for Billy Williams—Pueblo, Burlington, Fort Worth, San Antonio, Houston—before he finally made it with the Cubs. It took a while, and a couple of on-again off-again starts with the Cubs but when finally he had a chance as a regular in the Cub outfield he hit a grand-slam home run in his first important game. By season's end he'd batted .278 and was elected rookie of the year for 1961. It was the first—and, until now, last—award he was to get for his perfection.

Over the years, his skills remained high: he batted .300 or more three times, he outhomered slugger Ernie Banks for five consecutive years, he outproduced Johnny Bench in Bench's best year—Billy produced 224 runs in 1970 compared to Bench's 200 runs-produced. Within baseball, he was acknowledged the finest No. 3 hitter in the game—he could run so fast that he was tough to double-up with men on the bases, he could hit with consistency (over 200 hits in three different seasons), and he could hit with power. Most of all, he could hit in the clutch: with men on the bases, he is—and has been—one of the very few .400 hitters in baseball.

There was more. But Billy Williams had to make it more. For he turned out to be one of the few highly-gifted defensive players among the outfielders in the National League. It was not a natural gift; it was a cultivated one. In his first full year in professional baseball, Billy Williams committed 25 errors. "I remember the first game he ever played, he wound up on his stomach, trying to field a fly ball," said Don Biebel, his first manager at Ponca City. Ground balls were no better; he approached them like a mouse approaching a cat. On top of all that, he did not have a spectacularly strong arm. But all through his career—including his years in the majors—he labored to overcome these problems. To compensate for his arm, he learned to get the ball away quickly and with great accuracy—"I point my left foot and left leg at where I'm going to throw"—and then learned to follow through so that his throwing arm and shoulder (his right arm) were pointing at the target when he finished his motion. He learned not only to pick up the ground ball but to pick it up so that he'd always have his feet and body in exactly the right position to get off the throw. He spent hour after hour throwing a ball at short range against a brick wall—scooping it up and shifting to exactly the correct fielding-to-throwing position as it caromed off the wall, and then firing the ball back at a specific brick with his throw ... and scooping it up and shifting again from fielding into throwing positions, so tirelessly that at last the movements themselves became almost as reflexive as blinking. To learn to handle fly balls, he had first to learn how to get the jump on the ball as it comes off the bat; and that was a matter of looking not at the flight of the ball as it's being pitched but of staring at the strike zone at home plate—where the batter will be swinging—so that the left-fielder can see the ball either going through it or coming out of it just after impact. The style, tone, and amplitude of Billy Williams in applying these skills—particularly in tracking fly balls—was important not only to his incomparable consistency as an outfielder but to the success of Cub pitchers: he made spectacular catches of fly balls in three no-hit games—by Ken Holtzman, Burt

Hooten, and Milt Pappas—that meant the difference between the no-hitter and just another well-pitched ball game. Without Billy Williams, therefore, Holtzman, Hooten, and Pappas would not be in baseball's Hall of Fame.

As the years passed, his skills became surer and his outlook more mature. He married and had four daughters. He shifted his fishing enthusiasm from a stream that washes through pastureland not far from Whistler to some of the white-water rivers of the north country and Canada. He learned to pace himself: at times in his record-breaking string of consecutive games he became exhausted—and yet he kept on. He is the only player in baseball history to have played seven consecutive 162-game seasons without a game off. There were times when fatigue was so overwhelming that it warped his whole style of play. That was a profound lesson: when he was tempted to go for the triple crown in 1972—he held the batting lead and trailed only slightly in homers and RBI's—he decided instead to take a rest. "The batting title was what I wanted," he says. And the "reach" for the homer-title might send his swing so awry that he'd lose his lead in hitting.

To many, he's still a mystery—though his reknown is growing. ". . . He isn't easy to get close to," it was suggested in a Chicago newspaper last summer. "Definitely a case of 'still waters running deep,' he must do things on his own time, in his own way, for he's quite independent. He's also sensitive, unbiased, very psychic (or has prophetic dreams), versatile, moody, shrewd, idealistic, and dexterous, with the fantastic ability to make accurate, hairline decisions under pressure. . . .

". . . He's still reserved but when he opens up, he talks a blue streak. . . . He's comical in a kind of loony way, would probably make a great mimic because of his good ear for dialect and language, and has an unquenchable curiosity. He's well read, able to integrate the old with the new and has the rare capacity for synthesis . . . nervous exhaustion might be his worst enemy so he needs to be sure and have 'alone' time periodically to restore himself."

In the end, therefore, Billy Williams is not simply a machine but a man superbly within himself. He has hopes and ambitions and the ability to articulate them—though mostly to himself. Every season, when he walks into the

Cub clubhouse in the spring for the first time, he places a sealed envelope on—or under—the shelf in his locker. It has a piece of paper with his goals for himself stated in statistics: last season it was to hit .330, to get 120 RBI's, and to hit 40 home runs. He missed the home run mark but not the other two. What will the envelope predict this year?

BILLY WILLIAMS

Year	Club	Lea	Pos	AB	R	H	HR	RBI	Avg.
1956	Ponca City	Soon. St.	OF	17	4	4	0	4	.235
1957	Ponca City	Soon. St.	OF	451	87	140	17	95	.310
1958	Pueblo	Western	OF	80	9	20	2	11	.250
1958	Burlington	Three-I	OF	214	38	65	10	38	.304
1959	San Antonio	Texas	1B-OF	371	57	118	10	79	.318
1959	Ft. Worth	A. A.	OF	21	7	10	1	5	.476
1959	Chicago	N. L.	OF	33	0	5	0	2	.152
1960	Houston	A. A.	OF	473	74	153	26	80	.323
1960	Chicago	N. L.	OF	47	4	13	2	7	.277
1961	Chicago	N. L.	OF	529	75	147	25	86	.278
1962	Chicago	N. L.	OF	618	94	184	22	92	.298
1963	Chicago	N. L.	OF	612	87	175	25	95	.286
1964	Chicago	N. L.	OF	645	100	201	33	98	.312
1965	Chicago	N. L.	OF	645	115	203	34	108	.315
1966	Chicago	N. L.	OF	648	100	179	29	91	.276
1967	Chicago	N. L.	OF	634	92	176	28	84	.278
1968	Chicago	N. L.	OF	642	91	185	30	98	.288
1969	Chicago	N. L.	OF	642	103	188	21	95	.293
1970	Chicago	N. L.	OF	636	137	205	42	129	.322
1971	Chicago	N. L.	OF	594	86	179	28	93	.301
1972	Chicago	N. L.	OF	574	95	191	37	122	.333

WILBUR WOOD

All in The Knuckles

by WILLIAM BARRY FURLONG

There's a tooth missing in front but the gap in his mouth is usually concealed by a long cigar. He is not lean; he is not muscled; he throws the ball with the casual air of a father shooting baskets with his son in the backyard. His shirttail is always about to escape confinement and his wheat-colored hair decided, after three short decades of struggle for survival, to retreat to nothingness. To most folks, Wilbur Wood of the Chicago White Sox looks like in the words of Jack Griffin, the sports columnist of the Chicago Sun-Times—"the guy who just won the beer frame."

But the things that Wilbur Wood can do with a baseball a moth wouldn't believe. They could take lessons in evasive tactics from Wilbur's knuckleball. It has made him a 20-game winner for two years in a row—after years of anonymity—and has also made him a consistent contender for the AL's Cy Young Award. Last season, with a 24-17 record, he finished second to Gaylord Perry of Cleveland in the Cy Young balloting.

The remarkable thing is that he's done all this without a "major-league" fast ball or a "major-league" curve ball. All he has is that knuckleball, which he throws at least 75 percent of the time.

"When my knuckleball is working, there's nobody in the world that can beat me," he said. "When it's not working, there's nobody in the world I can beat."

It is not boastful. It's a matter of fact. For ol' Wilbur is a calm man, not given to preening or pride. He has a temperament as easy and relaxed as his pitching motion.

117

"There's no sense in being uptight about things," said Wilbur. "I'm a believer in the notion that if something's going to happen, it's going to happen. I just go out there and pitch and figure that it's a job that has to be done and it's got to be done to the best of my ability." If it comes up winners, that's wonderful. If it comes up losers, that's going to happen in a man's life, too.

"There's nothing I have to do for Wilbur," said pitching coach Johnny Sain of the White Sox, "except give him a ball before the game and give him a cigar after it."

It helps to have an indestructible temperament. Psychologically, the Cleveland Indians last year tried to retaliate on Wilbur for the White Sox hazing of pitcher Gaylord Perry: the Sox kept asking the umpires to shake Perry down to find just what—if anything—he was putting on the ball that made it behave so peculiarly and where he was hiding it. The umps never did find anything incriminating but the Indians decided that Wilbur's ball behaved mighty strangely, too, and—though they knew why—they figured it would be psychologically destructive to have Wilbur shaken down by the umps every few innings, too. ("Cut off his knuckles!" called out Indian third baseman Buddy Bell during one of his shakedowns.) That didn't bother Wilbur; contempt is an emotion beneath his abilities. He just went ahead, calmly and methodically, to whip the Indians pretty much as he pleased.

The physical hazards are more pronounced—and sometimes more painful. Wilbur gives up a lot of home runs if that knuckler doesn't quite knuckle—he was tagged for 28 of them last year. One homer came in the opening game of the season, with two out in the ninth, and deprived the White Sox of a much-desired win as a symbol of their new-found winning image. The same thing happened again in mid-August, with Wood seeking to become the first 20-game winner in the majors: Brant Alyea—who had been playing in Des Moines the previous weekend—hit a ninth-inning homer for the Oakland A's to wipe out a 1-0 win of the White Sox. But ol' Wilbur wasn't about to fall prey to being "psyched" by his own previous failure. This time he kicked the mound for a while, uttered a few unholy incantations and settled down to work again. He wound up pitching 11 innings that day, the longest he'd ever pitched, gave up only two hits. And won the game, 3-1.

The unbelievable thing—now that he's won so much so

easily—is that it took so long for anybody in baseball to understand about Wilbur and the gift that he possesses. That was the reason he was in his 12th season of professional baseball before he had a 20-win season—and that was the reason he almost quit baseball altogether.

In the beginning, he wasn't thinking baseball at all. He was thinking hockey and he was going to become that *rara avis* of professional sports—a left-handed goalie. For he was growing up in the hockey-mad environs of Boston—today he makes his home in Cambridge, the seat of Harvard and Al Capp and other illustrious contradictions—and he was inevitably pulled towards the game of his times. He played baseball because it was *there* and he learned to pitch the knuckleball because he made a mistake. He was 12 years old and he was trying to imitate his father's palm ball, which, like the knuckler, moves towards the plate without rotating. Because he couldn't envelope the ball in his hands, he threw something that turned out to be a knuckler. It had an engaging unpredictability but it wasn't what you'd throw to attract a big-league baseball scout—"They look to see if you've got *velocity*," says Wilbur, "and they sign you if it looks like you do." Wilbur had enough velocity to look good in high school baseball—if not in the major leagues—but he kept tinkering with the knuckler, if only for survival's sake.

When he was 15, and in ninth-grade, he was pitching a semi-pro league in Belmont, Massachusetts, and he remembers how one of the hoary old ex-pros on another team tried to con him out of using that "fool pitch." But his success, with the "fool pitch" and the others was great enough to persuade the Boston Red Sox to sign him—and to give him three unsuccessful chances to make the big-league team. Then they unloaded him on Pittsburgh, which ignored him for two seasons—he was the pitcher-of-record in only four games—and then sent him back to the minor leagues. That's when the White Sox picked him up.

That's also when Wilbur almost quit baseball. He figured: "I could be a good triple-A ballplayer the rest of my life or I could get out of baseball." He talked it over with his wife, Sandy, and she asked him the pointed question: "Do you think you've given baseball your full shot?" He decided to take one last swing at it. "It was obvious that I wasn't going to stick in the big time on the strength of my fast ball and my curve. I hadn't been using my knuckleball much and I thought maybe I ought to give it a shot."

With the White Sox he had the chance. They assigned him to the bullpen, along with old knuckleball hurler Hoyt Wilhelm. The knuckler was a relief pitcher's specialty: most batters are so accustomed to the rhythm of the fast-ball, breaking-ball that the knuckler leaves them lurching drunkenly with their eyeballs hanging out and their bats waving as futilely as a man trying to swat gnats with a redwood tree. Hoyt was a right-hander and Wilbur was a left-hander and the two of them combined to drive White Sox opponents cross-eyed with frustration. Wilbur set a club record for appearances (88) in 1968 and he relieved in 241 games over a three-year-period, winning 32 games—or more than any other pitcher on the ball club.

But to Wilbur Wood, the value and the opportunity was wound up in the presence and insight of Hoyt Wilhelm. "Hoyt could tell what I was doing wrong, just by the way the ball moved," says Wilbur. "When I made a bad pitch, he could tell me exactly what I was doing wrong and how to correct for it." Out of all this came an important skill: "I can throw this pitch for strikes," says Wilbur. He does not know exactly how it's going to break—any more than the batter does—but he figures it's going to break through the strike zone. Which means the batter has to swing and—often—miss. Or that he has to sit back and wait and take a called strike.

In 1971, the White Sox sent Wilbur back to the bullpen—as always—and then had second thoughts: they lost one starting pitcher through injury, others through misfeasance and finally they turned to Wilbur as their No. 4 starter. By season's end, he was one of the premier pitchers in the American League: he'd won 22 games as a starter, had a 1.91 earned-run average.

There was in all this—and the success that was to come—much of the old bullpen artist in Wilbur Wood. "I'm still a relief pitcher at heart, pitching one batter at a time, rather than one game at a time," he said last summer. It didn't bother him how often he pitched: he worked often with two days rest, instead of three, and there was talk that he might start—and win—a double-header. "An old bullpen pitcher never has to worry about rest," he said. "You're ready to go all the time." And he didn't worry over the game, or the team, he was suddenly to face. "A relief pitcher handles each batter like it could cost him the game," he says. "A starter can fool around if he has a lead but a relief pitcher is looking down the gun muzzle almost every time."

Because of Wilbur's attitude, and his skills, the White Sox were able to do something almost unprecedented in modern baseball: they set up a three-man starting rotation last season, instead of the customary four or five-man rotation. That meant that the White Sox starters—principally Wood, Stan Bahnsen, and Tom Bradley—would have to work with only two days of rest between each start, instead of three. The one man who was proven in all this was Wood: he had done it often in 1971 and at one point in early 1972 worked four games in ten days. It was not, as it happened, a discipline that endured without change through the entire season: about half the time, manager Chuck Tanner had a fourth starter ready to rotate with his "Great Trio." But the success of the "quick-start" men was so pronounced that, among them, they were the winning pitchers 61 times ... out of the 87 games won by the White Sox.

The quick-start system was not new to the White Sox strategy corps: pitching coach Johnny Sain had helped hurl the old Boston Braves to a pennant in 1948 by working nine consecutive starts with only two days of rest between each one. (He doesn't remember that he won them all—but he does remember that he finished them all.)

"Most mature pitchers should thrive when they pitch with only two days' rest," says manager Chuck Tanner. But even that concept has its limitations—as Wood's record in 1972 suggests. In those games where he had three days' of rest between starts, Wilbur was 12-7 with an earned-run average of 2.40. In the two-day's-rest rotation, he was 12-10 with an ERA of 2.62. Actually he was a better pitcher, for most of the season, on two day's rest than with three day's rest. For his decline in effectiveness, on the two-day-rotation, took place in the late stages of the season. He was the first pitcher in the major leagues to win 20 games last year: his 20th win came on August 12, when there were six-to-seven weeks left in the season and 47 games left on the White Sox schedule. If he pitched in one-third of them, he'd have 15 or 16 starts and a good chance to win 30 games or more. But he slowed down: he won his 24th game on September 7 and never won his 25th, despite seven tries at it.

"I wish I could say that I was tired—but I'm not," he said. "I'd love to say that I had a sore arm, but I don't." All he could say was that his knuckler wasn't working as well as it had been. Whether it was the strain of the quick-start rotation is hard to tell, at least from the way that Wilbur felt. But the figures suggest that—as manager Tanner indicates—he did thrive on the quick-start rotation, but only up to late August. He was even better with two-day's rest at that point than he was with three-day's rest.

The trick of knowing when Wilbur is less-than-sharp is watching his bases-on-balls—and even the ball-and-strike count. He pitched more than anybody else in the league last year—376⅔ innings—but he gave up only 74 walks. That's an average of only 1.7 per game. So when Wilbur starts issuing four or five walks a game you know he's in trouble. For much of the secret of Wood's success is based on his ability to throw strikes—but not strikeouts. His goal is to throw only 85 to 105 pitches a game; that keeps the knuckler so fresh and erratic—in the perspective of the batter—that it remains effective.

Why don't more pitchers turn to the knuckler like Wilbur?

"It's because most of them start to come up with it at the end of their careers," says Wood. "They lose a little off their fast ball and all of a sudden they think they're going to the knuckler.

"It just won't work that way. If you already threw a knuckler that was good but you didn't know why, or if you threw one that was bad and you didn't know why, then I'd say 'Yes. Maybe.'

"Take me. I was throwing the knuckleball in junior high school. ... When I had to decide on a new pitch, it was one I already had for seven years. Where else you going to work on a new pitch? In triple-A ball? What if it doesn't work—where are you then?"

Not in the major leagues, most likely. In the minors, with no fast ball and no curve and trying to get by on a pitch that few managers—outside of the likes of Chuck Tanner—much care for.

How long does it take to control the knuckler?

Wilbur doesn't know. "I just aim for the middle, belt high. Sometimes it breaks in," he says. "Sometimes it breaks away. Sometimes it breaks somewhere else."

There are limitations to all this, of course. Not even Wood can work all the time. And not simply because of his arm; there is also the matter of the effectiveness of the knuckler. Tanner was asked whether—with a four-game series against Oakland about to come up, and with first place at stake—he'd use Wood in two games: the first and the fourth. No, said Tanner. Not because Wood would get tired. "But one of the assets of the knuckle ball is that it comes in as a strange pitch to every team you meet," he said. "If you use it in one game, and then use it again in the same series, the batters might get used to it—get onto the rhythm—and you'd lose one of the reasons it's so effective."

Even with these limitations, the expectations arising out of the skills of Wilbur Wood have given a new dimension to pitching. It takes little to perceive that—if he continues on a two-day rest basis for most or all of a season—he will get enough additional starts to think in terms of a 30-win season, not merely a 20-win season. He may not only win 30 games in a season soon. But with the quick-start rotation he'll get more starts than ever and with more muscle in the White Sox batting order he'll get more wins. Last year the White Sox scored only 28 more runs than did their opposition and yet that very thin edge—which averaged out to .18 runs per game more for the White Sox—was converted by the pitchers into 20 more wins than losses.

Wood tends to pitch low-run games: in his two-days' rest record last year, he pitched 11 games in which he gave up no-runs or one-run; he pitched 14 games in which he gave up two or less runs. The irony: he lost four of those games and went to a no-decision another time. So just a very small increase in run-production by the White Sox last year might have catapulted Wilbur Wood into the 30-win bracket.

The 30-win season is a rarity in itself; only Denny McLain (then with Detroit) has accomplished it in recent years—in 1968; and only three other men have done it in the last 50 years; Dizzy Dean with the St. Louis Cardinals in 1934, Lefty Grove with the Philadelphia A's in 1931, and Jim Bagby of the Cleveland Indians back in 1920. But it is within reach of Wilbur Wood: with the new dimensions to pitching rotations—the short-rest system—and a few more runs out of the White Sox power structure, he might become a one-man dynasty that will rewrite baseball history by the mid-1970's.

The one man who wouldn't get excited about all this is Wilbur Wood. He's an easy man—with records, or without them. Last year, he could have set several club records by starting and winning one more game—he would have become the winningest White Sox pitcher in 50 years if he'd gotten that 25th win. But once the pennant race was over, manager Tanner asked him—and a half-dozen other players—if they'd like to take the last few days of the season off. Wilbur said, "Yup."

So he gave up the last start, and perhaps the last win, and went home to his family. That's the way it is with Wilbur. An easy man who enjoys himself. He does what he can today—and tomorrow? ... well, the best is yet to come. For his is a world of easy grace and humor. Pitching is difficult at times, so is living, but there is no sense railing against the one or the other when you can talk softly, throw well and inhale the joy of a long cigar.

WILBUR WOOD

Year	Club	Lea	IP	W	L	SO	BB	H	ERA
1960	Waterloo	Midwest	20	1	0	21	9	20	2.70
1960	Raleigh	Carolina	77	3	5	59	32	85	3.84
1961	Winston-Salem	Carolina	111	8	5	103	33	99	3.15
1961	Boston	A. L.	13	0	0	7	7	14	5.54
1961	Johnstown	Eastern	74	3	7	44	15	80	4.62
1962	York	Eastern	219	15	11	178	62	198	2.84
1962	Boston	A. L.	8	0	0	3	3	6	3.38
1963	Seattle	P. C.	64	5	2	43	10	54	1.13
1963	Boston	A. L.	65	0	5	28	13	67	3.74
1964	Boston	A. L.	6	0	0	5	3	13	16.50
1964	Seattle	P. C.	211	15	8	197	49	176	2.30
1964	Pittsburgh	N. L.	17	0	2	7	11	16	3.71
1965	Pittsburgh	N. L.	51	1	1	29	16	44	3.18
1966	Columbus	Int.	224	14	8	109	38	197	2.41
1967	Chicago	A. L.	95	4	2	47	28	95	2.46
1968	Chicago	A. L.	159	13	12	74	33	127	1.87
1969	Chicago	A. L.	120	10	11	73	40	113	3.00
1970	Chicago	A. L.	122	9	13	85	36	118	2.80
1971	Chicago	A. L.	334	22	13	210	62	272	1.91
1972	Chicago	A. L.	376	24	17	193	74	325	2.53

FINAL STANDINGS—1972

AMERICAN LEAGUE
Eastern Division

	W	L	Pct.	GB
Detroit	86	70	.551	—
Boston	85	70	.548	½
Baltimore	80	74	.519	5
New York	76	79	.510	6½
Cleveland	72	84	.462	14
Milwaukee	65	91	.417	22

Western Division

	W	L	Pct.	GB
Oakland	93	62	.600	—
Chicago	87	67	.565	5½
Minnesota	77	77	.500	15½
Kansas City	76	78	.494	16½
California	75	80	.484	18
Texas	54	100	.351	38½

NATIONAL LEAGUE
Eastern Division

	W	L	Pct.	GB
Pittsburgh	96	59	.619	—
Chicago	85	70	.548	11
New York	83	73	.532	13½
St. Louis	75	81	.481	21½
Montreal	70	86	.449	26½
Philadelphia	59	97	.378	37½

Western Division

	W	L	Pct.	GB
Cincinnati	95	59	.617	—
Houston	84	69	.549	10½
Los Angeles	85	70	.548	10½
Atlanta	70	84	.455	25
San Francisco	69	86	.445	26½
San Diego	58	95	.379	36½

WORLD SERIES—1972

GAME-BY-GAME

FIRST GAME

```
Oakland    _____  0 2 0   0 1 0   0 0 0—3   4   0
Cincinnati _____  0 1 0   1 0 0   0 0 0—2   7   0
```
Holtzman, Fingers (6), Blue (7) and Tenace; Nolan, Borbon (7), Carroll (8) and Bench.
Home runs—Oakland: Tenace (2). Attendance: 52, 918

SECOND GAME

```
Oakland    _____  0 1 1   0 0 0   0 0 0—2   9   1
Cincinnati _____  0 0 0   0 0 0   0 0 1—1   6   0
```
Hunter, Fingers (9) and Tenace; Grimsley, Borbon (6), Hall (8) and Bench.
Home runs—Oakland: Rudi. Attendance 53,224

THIRD GAME

```
Cincinnati _____  0 0 0   0 0 0   1 0 0—1   4   2
Oakland    _____  0 0 0   0 0 0   0 0 0—0   3   2
```
Billingham, Carroll (9) and Bench; Odom, Blue (8), Fingers (8) and Tenace.
Attendance: 49,410

FOURTH GAME

```
Cincinnati _____  0 0 0   0 0 0   0 2 0—2   7   1
Oakland    _____  0 0 0   0 1 0   0 0 2—3  10   1
```
Gullet, Borbon (8), Carroll (9) and Bench; Holtzman, Blue (8), Fingers (9) and Tenace.
Home runs—Oakland, Tenace. Attendance: 49,410

FIFTH GAME

```
Cincinnati _____  1 0 0   1 1 0   0 1 1—5   8   0
Oakland    _____  0 3 0   1 0 0   0 0 0—4   7   2
```
McGlothlin, Borbon (4), Hall (5), Carroll (7), Grimsley (8), Billingham (9) and Bench; Hunter, Fingers (5), Hamilton (9) and Tenace.
Home runs—Cincinnati, Rose 1, Menke 1; Oakland, Tenace 4. Attendance: 49,410

SIXTH GAME

```
Oakland    _____  0 0 0   0 1 0   0 0 0—1   7   1
Cincinnati _____  1 1 1   0 0 1   5 0 x—8  10   0
```
Blue, Locker (5), Hamilton (7), Horlen (7) and Tenace; Nolan, Grimsley (5), Borbon (6), Hall (7) and Bench.
Home runs—Cincinnati, Bench 1. Attendance: 52,737

SEVENTH GAME

```
Oakland    _____  1 0 0   0 0 2   0 0 0—3   6   1
Cincinnati _____  0 0 0   0 1 0   0 1 0—2   4   2
```
Odom, Hunter (5), Holtzman (8), Fingers (8) and Duncan; Billingham, Borbon (6), Carroll (6), Grimsley (7), Hall (8) and Bench.
Attendance: 56,040

ATHLETICS vs. REDS

WORLD SERIES—1972 COMPOSITE

CINCINNATI REDS

	AB	R	H	2B	3B	HR	RBI	B.AV.
Rose, lf	28	3	6	0	0	1	2	.214
Morgan, 2b	24	4	3	2	0	0	1	.125
Tolan, cf	26	2	7	1	0	0	6	.269
Bench, c	23	4	6	1	0	1	1	.261
Perez, 1b	23	3	10	2	0	0	2	.435
Menke, 3b	24	1	2	0	0	1	2	.083
Geronimo, rf	19	1	3	0	0	0	3	.158
McRae, rf-ph	9	1	4	1	0	0	2	.444
Foster, pr-rf	0	0	0	0	0	0	0	.000
Concepcion, ss-ph	13	2	4	0	1	0	2	.308
Chaney, ss-ph	7	0	0	0	0	0	0	.000
Nolan, p	3	0	0	0	0	0	0	.000
Borbon, p	0	0	0	0	0	0	0	.000
Uhlaender, ph	4	0	1	1	0	0	0	.000
Carroll, p	0	0	0	0	0	0	0	.000
Javier, ph	2	0	0	0	0	0	0	.000
Grimsley, p	2	0	0	0	0	0	0	.000
Hague, ph-rf	3	0	0	0	0	0	0	.000
Hall, p	2	0	0	0	0	0	0	.000
Billingham, p	5	0	0	0	0	0	0	.000
Gullett, p	2	0	0	0	0	0	0	.000
McGlothlin, p	1	0	0	0	0	0	0	.000
Totals	220	21	46	8	1	3	21	.209

OAKLAND ATHLETICS

	AB	R	H	2B	3B	HR	RBI	B.AV.
Campaneris, ss	28	1	5	0	0	0	0	.179
Rudi, lf	25	1	6	0	0	1	1	.240
Alou, rf	24	0	1	0	0	0	0	.042
Epstein, 1b	16	1	0	0	0	0	0	.000
Lewis, pr	0	2	0	0	0	0	0	.000
Hegan, 1b-ph	5	0	1	0	0	0	0	.200
Bando, 3b	26	2	7	1	0	0	1	.269
Hendrick, cf	15	3	2	0	0	0	0	.133
Tenace, c-1b	23	5	6	1	0	4	9	.348
Green, 2b	18	0	6	2	0	0	1	.333
Marquez, ph	5	0	3	0	0	0	1	.600
Kublak, 2b	3	0	1	0	0	0	0	.333
Holtzman, p	5	0	0	0	0	0	0	.000
Fingers, p	1	0	0	0	0	0	0	.000
Blue, p	1	0	0	0	0	0	0	.000
Hunter, p	5	0	1	0	0	0	1	.200
Odom, p-pr	4	0	0	0	0	0	0	.000
Mincher, ph	1	0	1	0	0	0	1	1.000
Mangual, ph-cf	10	1	3	0	0	0	1	.300
Hamilton, p	0	0	0	0	0	0	0	.000
Duncan, ph-c	5	0	1	0	0	0	0	.200
Locker, p	0	0	0	0	0	0	0	.000
Horlen, p	0	0	0	0	0	0	0	.000
Totals	220	16	46	4	0	5	16	.209

PITCHING

REDS

	G	IP	H	R	ER	BB	SO	ERA
Nolan (0-1)	2	10⅔	7	4	4	2	3	3.27
Borbon (0-1)	6	7	7	3	3	2	4	3.86
Carroll (0-1)	5	5⅔	6	1	1	4	3	1.50
Grimsley (2-1)	4	7	7	2	2	3	2	2.57
Hall	4	8⅓	6	0	0	2	7	0.00
Billingham (1-0)	3	13⅔	6	1	0	4	11	0.00
Gullett	1	7	5	1	1	2	4	1.29
McGlothlin	1	3	2	4	4	2	3	12.00
Totals	7	62⅓	46	16	15	21	37	2.18

Saves—Carroll, Billingham, Hall.

ATHLETICS

	G	IP	H	R	ER	BB	SO	ERA
Holtzman (1-0)	3	12⅔	11	3	3	3	4	2.08
Fingers (1-1)	6	10⅓	4	2	2	4	10	1.80
Hunter (2-0)	3	16	12	5	5	6	10	2.81
Odom (0-1)	2	11⅓	5	2	2	6	13	1.64
Hamilton	2	1⅓	3	4	4	1	1	36.00
Blue	4	8⅔	8	4	4	5	5	4.15
Locker	1	⅓	1	0	0	0	0	0.00
Horlen	1	1⅓	2	1	1	2	1	9.00
Totals	7	62	46	21	21	27	44	3.05

SCORE BY INNINGS

OAKLAND	1	6	1	1	3	2	0	0	2—16
CINCINNATI	1	1	0	3	3	1	6	4	2—21

E—Bench, Morgan, Perez, Tolan, Concepcion, Epstein 2, Hunter, Tenace, Holtzman, Alou, Bando, Mangual, Campaneris. DP—Cincinnati 5, Oakland 4. LOB—Cincinnati 49, Oakland 45. SB—Rose, Morgan 2, Tolan 5, Bench 2, Geronimo, Concepcion, Alou. S—Menke, 2, Concepcion, Javier, Grimsley, Campaneris 2, Alou, Hendrick, Fingers, Mangual. SF—Concepcion, McRae, Perez. HBP—by McGlothlin, Rudi; by Fingers, Chaney. WP—Blue, Fingers, Horlen, Hunter.